This Book I:

My two daughters, Claire and Angela
Thank you for making me the happiest mum in the world.
You are both the most amazing, loving daughters.

My mum and late dad
Thank you mum for bringing me into this world and sorry for all the times I made you worry and cry.
Dad, you were the greatest man I have ever known.
Thank you for being my dad and my guardian angel.

My partner, Ronnie
Thank you for your love, patience and encouragement while I wrote this book.

To all cancer patents and survivors
Never ever give up.

My Lucky Break

Chapter One

I opened my eyes. The bright sunshine was streaming through the window, I was in bed in a medium size room I did not recognise. The room was painted white and had a very sterile look about it; the only furniture I could see was a teak cupboard in line with my head next to the left side of my bed. I saw my husband Mathew sitting on the bed next to me, wearing his favourite grey shirt and his Wrangler jeans, his shiny black hair freshly washed. When I focus my eyes on his face he was looking at me in a way I had never seen him look before and there were tears in his beautiful deep brown eyes.

There was another man in the room, standing at the bottom of my bed. He was tall, of a slim build but not skinny. He had light brown hair and very attractive features, with stunning blue eyes. I would say he was older than me, possibly mid 40's, and he seemed to be smiling at me. He was wearing a smart pair of black trousers that had been pressed with a sharp edged crease down the centre of both legs and a white open coat that he was wearing over a pale blue shirt.

I looked around me and wondered where I was. This was not my bedroom and then it struck me, this was a hospital room and I was in a hospital bed.

I was lying flat on my back. I glanced down and saw I was wearing a hospital gown and there was a tube connected to my left hand. Following the tube up above my head I could see a bag filled with fluid attached to a stand and it was dripping into the tube that was travelling down to my hand.

Matthew was holding my other hand, very gently caressing it with his thumb. I started to open my mouth to speak but the tall man at the bottom of my bed spoke before me. He said, "Lisa, please do not move and Happy New Year, welcome to the year 2000."

What was going on? I couldn't remember celebrating the big New Year's Eve party. The Millennium year 2000, the turn of the first year of the 21st century that everyone had been talking about for the past year. The fireworks lighting up the sky, popping champagne bottles at midnight and waiting to see if all the computers in the world would crash.

He spoke again and said "Lisa, I am Michael Tremblay I am a Doctor. Don't be alarmed, you are in hospital, you are in the Willow Royal Hospital in Corby. You are here because you had an accident. Do you remember any of it?"

Chapter Two

29th December 1999 and it was a beautiful morning. It had put down about a foot of snow through the night and everywhere looked just like a Christmas card that was covered in glitter. We were in a place called Jasper, a small town in the heart of Jasper National Park in Alberta, Canada. Some call it the gentle giant of the Rockies. It's a rustic little place with an authentic mountain community that are very friendly.

About a hundred years ago it was a popular fur trading post, then the railway was built and in 1913 it was named Jasper, where a community was born and stone and timber was used to make the historical treasures you see throughout the town today. It's a popular place for tourists especially with the Rocky Mountaineer train that stops there as it takes you through the beautiful mountains all the way to Vancouver and of course there's the winter skiing. Not to forget the tan-coloured animals with white patches on the rears with fabulous racks of antlers, the elk.

They roam through the town and streets as if they own the place it's a fantastic sight, one I had never seen before.

Mathew and I arrived here yesterday with our two good friends Doug and Kathy. They had flown over the day after Boxing Day from England to stay with us in our home in Corby and celebrate the Millennium New Year together.

We had not seen Doug and Kathy for a couple of years after we emigrated to Canada from the UK with my daughters Melissa, 18, and Jessica, 16, and Melissa's boyfriend Graeme. We arrived on 1st July 1998, to our surprise Canada Day one of biggest Bank Holidays of the year. The pilot on the flight invited us to the cockpit just as we were flying over Canada from the Hudson Bay. He signed his flight route sheet with all the air space we had flown through and gave it to us as a memento of our flight. We framed it and hung it on the wall in our new house.

Melissa, Jessica and Graeme returned to England to stay with family and friends to enjoy a Millennium New Year party and Melissa and Graeme had another celebration of their own to attend. They flew back to the UK the same day Doug and Kathy arrived.

Matthew and I had bought new skis for Christmas and were desperate to try them out so he wasn't going to say no when I suggested we all go skiing to Jasper.

With the hotel booked, we all piled into Matthews truck and excitedly set off on the 380 kilometre drive, which would take us about three and a half hours, stopping about half way in Matlock for lunch. Approaching Jasper was great fun. Matthew dodged the elk on the streets and we kept our eyes peeled for any sighting of large moose. After checking into our hotel, it was time to explore the historical town and hire sets of skis for Doug and Kathy.

We laughed so much at the funny stories the locals were telling us in the Whistle Stop Pub which had such a welcoming atmosphere and good beer.

What a beautiful morning it was with all the fresh snow. The temperature was -15c, we were lucky because at this time of year it can be really cold, dropping well below -30c. We stood inside the entrance of the hotel waiting for Matthew to clear the truck of snow that had covered it overnight and to warm up the inside for our 20 minutes' drive south out of Jasper.

Good job we were in a 4 x 4 as the roads still had a covering of snow even though the snowplough had been along to clear the bulk of it. After leaving the Icefields Parkway for the 93A we looked for Marmot Road, which would lead us up the winding snow covered road to Marmot Basin, the most beautiful alpine ski area you have ever seen.

It looked like one big winter playground with people dressed in all different colours, skiing and snowboarding at the base of the ski hill. There were adults and children, some waiting in the queue for the snow lifts while others were having fun throwing snowballs and falling over.

With the sun still shining, it was perfect for our day of excitement and thrills. Matthew parked the truck outside the entrance so we could go into the reception to buy our daily passes and, as Kathy had never skied before, we booked her in for lessons.

Mathew and Doug were very good skiers, with lots of confidence, whereas I was pretty average and stayed well clear of the black runs. Matthew drove the truck further up the mountain to one of the car parks and we all piled out excited and, after getting our boots and skis on, we were ready for some fun.

Kathy went for her lesson and we headed for the ski lifts. To ease us in gently, the three of us rode the Express Quad chair lift to the mid-mountain area where we could ski the easy runs. The snow conditions were good and, after a few easy runs, Mathew and Doug skied a couple of the black runs while I stuck to where I was feeling more comfortable. When we met up again, Matthew said it was time we got higher up the ski hill so we took the Express Quad chair lift then skied across to the Eagle Ridge chair lift which took us up higher, to the east side of the mountain. The chair lift doesn't stop when it gets to the top. It just moves very low to the ground so you can ease yourself out of the chair and ski a few metres before you come to a stop. I moved to the edge of the chair waiting until my skis touched the ground and, with my ski poles ready, I shuffled off the chair as ladylike as I could but went off balance, tumbling into both Matthew and Doug and we all ended up in a heap, to the great amusement of everyone.

The views from there were spectacular, looking down over the tops of the pine trees. The run down from there was lovely and I had skied it many times in the past. It's more difficult than the runs I had skied in the morning so I had to concentrate and put all my skiing skills into action. Of course the guys were ahead of me, setting off at a faster pace and weaving in and out of the tree line runs that had been groomed to perfection. My heart was beating fast and with the adrenaline running through my body it was invigorating. The guys were waiting for me half way down on a level piece of the run, snapping away taking pictures of me with their cameras as I skied up towards them. I was desperate for a drink so we headed for the mid mountain chalet in the distance then, realising it was time to meet Kathy from her lessons, we skied the rest of the way down to the bottom of the hill.

Kathy was so pleased to see us and she couldn't stop talking about her morning, how good looking the ski instructor was, how many times she fell over and how fast the little kids had zoomed past her. It was great to hear the excitement in her voice.

She couldn't wait to go up the mountain with us to try out her new skills so we all agreed we would do one run with Kathy then stop for lunch. We skied across to the express chair lift and luckily we could all get in one chair. This was Kathy's first time on ski lifts as she had been using the school chair with the instructor all morning.

Safely off the lift, we gathered together telling Kathy about the run we planned to ski down. Kathy was so excited as we set off at a nice gentle pace. I stayed alongside her while we skied west, heading down towards the bend and then onto an easy run to the bottom while the guys were skiing from side to side, showing off. We'd have laughed so much if they had fallen over.

We were all in need of warm drinks by now but Doug wanted to go back up with Kathy, back up to do the same run together so Matthew and I headed for the Caribou Chalet which was located at the base of the ski area.

It was lovely and warm inside the chalet and we sat beside a log fire enjoying a big mug of hot chocolate. When Doug and Kathy joined us we enjoyed a well-earned lunch of burger and fries while we all talked about our morning on the slopes.

Chapter Three

I looked at Matthew then back to Dr Tremblay and asked, "An accident? What do you mean? What accident?"

I felt aware of my body and could feel something tight around the upper part of it. I put my chin down and my hospital gown was lying loosely across me with the sheets on the bed folded down just covering my legs. I could see under the gown and was alarmed when I saw a yellow rigid plastic structure covered in little holes wrapped around the whole of the upper part of my body going from my neck down to my pelvis. I had never seen anything like it before.

The tears were welling up in my eyes then starting to trickle down my cheek. I started to panic, wondering what was wrong with me.

Releasing my right hand from Matthews's grip I slowly moved my arms and legs, first by lifting my arm off the bed then watching as I made my left arm move. I moved both my legs one at a time slightly to the side with my heel running along the bed sheet. Thinking if I 'm able to move my arms and legs, it will mean I am not paralysed. Dr Tremblay's voice stopped me. "Lisa I do not want you to move. You have had an accident and you have a serious back injury. You have fractured your third lumber spinal vertebrae in the lower back portion of your spinal column. We have fitted a brace called a clamshell and it's a device that wraps around your back, chest and stomach." It was there to protect my spine and stop me from bending forward or backwards and keeping me from twisting from side to side. He said it would help my spine to heal. There was a cannula inserted into my left hand, so they could give me fluids and medication straight into my blood stream.

All this information had me confused. It was making me agitated. I could not remember injuring my back, let alone having an accident. I did not want Dr Tremblay to say another word, I wanted him to leave and let me be on my own with my husband so I shouted at him to go. Dr Tremblay looked at Matthew then back to me and walked out of the door.

Chapter Four

I asked Matthew to tell me what had happened to me. "Lisa, "he said," we were having lunch in the chalet restaurant at Marmot Basin after a morning of skiing with Doug and Kathy." I could remember that, having so much fun, laughing as Kathy asking for chips with her burger and the girl behind the counter gave her a packet of potato crisps. Kathy didn't know that chips in England are fries in Canada.

He continued saying that after lunch we left the chalet. Kathy was feeling so good about her skiing she wanted to challenge herself and ski the big run we had done in the morning.

A bit ambitious for her first day of skiing, but Kathy was a very sporty and fit woman so, after putting our hats, gloves and goggles back on, we skied over to the Express Quad chair where we waited in line to board the ski lift.

The temperature had dropped and after an hour or so of sitting in front of that lovely log fire we were feeling the cold, the sun was beginning to vanish behind a cloud and it was starting to snow. We were all excited as we stood there holding our hands out to catch the big snowflakes. Doug and Kathy never see much snow back in England, living in the beautiful Lake District, they get more rain than snow.

As we were going up the mountain on the chair lift we could see people skiing down the ski runs beneath us, all going at different speeds. Once we were off the lift we skied slowly across the hill to the base of the next lift, the Eagle Ridge chair. There weren't many people waiting for this lift so it didn't take long until we were all sitting in line heading higher up the mountain. Looking down, I could see the treetops weren't as clear as they had been in the morning or from the lift we had just come off and the chair was swaying a little from side to side, which Doug found very funny but I had a very uneasy feeling about it.

I managed to leave the chair lift and stay on my feet this time, but Kathy was not so lucky and ended up in a heap on the ground, laughing as Doug pulled her upright onto her skies.

We all stood together, now starting to feel the cold. The wind had whipped up and the snow was coming down in big flakes and, with the breeze, it was coming at us at an angle. Looking ahead, the ski run was not very clear and we all knew this was going to be a difficult ski.

Matthew had heard one of the lift operators say on his radio that the lift was to close until the heavy snowstorm passed. Feeling uneasy, we all set off skiing close to each other with the guys in front so Kathy and I could follow them.

Coming down from the top was the tricky part as the visibility was very poor. I looked at Kathy and she looked as nervous as I felt. This was so wrong: poor Kathy experiencing this on her first day skiing.

I had such a bad feeling about this and couldn't wait until we were all safely down. Matthew shouted back at us to tell us to be careful and to stop when we reached the Eagle Chalet mid-way down the mountain. It didn't take us long to ski off the top even though we were struggling to see where we were going. The heavy snow and now strong wind was turning it into a white out and I kept losing sight of the guys in front of us and I was afraid for Kathy's safety, I didn't have experience skiing in these conditions let alone her.

Approaching the trees it became a little easier for us to see as they lined the run and we now had Matthew and Doug in sight. I was starting to feel a bit safer knowing that the worst part of the run was behind us.

When we arrived at the chalet all I wanted to do was get the hell off that mountain and finish skiing for the day, jump into Matthews's truck and head back into Jasper to the Whistle Stop Pub where we could all have a drink.

Outside the chalet, we grouped together from the wind and Matthew checked we were all feeling ok to continue, Doug and Kathy wanted to go inside and have a warm drink and wait for the snow to clear but I insisted we carry on skiing to the bottom, I wasn't sure the snow was going to stop any time today and we could always come back tomorrow as we had a two day pass.

Matthew was not happy with me, telling me I wasn't thinking about Kathy but I was so determined to carry on. Doug and Kathy, not wanting the day to be spoilt by Matthew and I falling out, agreed we should ski the rest of the way down, so we all set off again.

This part of the run is normally easy to ski but with these snow conditions we still needed to be careful. The fresh snow felt good under the skis but the visibility was still very poor. We were skiing out of the bend, dropping quite steeply then levelling off. Matthew led the way with Doug behind him and Kathy was behind me.

I glanced round to check Kathy was ok and, with twisting my body, my skis moved to the right then they struck a bump in the snow and I took off, flying through the air out of control. As my skis hit the ground they flipped me into a summersault, my head hit the ground first then I landed on my back, crashing into a snow bank.

I remember the pain being unbearable. I thought I had hurt my hips as that seemed to be where the pain was coming from. I tried to move but the pain made it impossible. Kathy and Doug were standing over me while Matthew was on his knees next to me telling me not to move.

They stopped a passing skier and Matthew asked him to ski down to the base of the mountain and inform the snow patrol and to tell them I was in so much pain and struggling to breathe. Matthew was constantly telling me not to move and that I would be ok, but the anxious look on his face had me worried.

It seemed to take ages until the snow patrol arrived but, in reality, it wasn't very long at all. Two men arrived on a snowmobile pulling a stretcher and a large medical bag. They quickly assessed my condition, realised how serious it was and radioed for an ambulance.

Without moving my head, they put a collar around my neck. Matthew was constantly telling them to be careful. He was very upset and getting angry because they didn't have any oxygen with them to help my breathing or anything for the pain. Matthew used to be a member of the mountain rescue team when we lived in the English Lake District and, naturally, he wanted to take charge but the snow patrol kept asking him to step back and let them do their job. They knew what they were doing and within minutes, they very gently slid a long spinal board under my back to stabilise me. They then moved me onto a long sledge, carefully secured by straps. Matthew insisted on helping strap me into the sledge and one of the men attached ropes from the sledge to the snow mobile and started pulling the sledge but it was going too fast and I was screaming in pain so they removed the rope from the snow mobile and Matthew and one of the other snow patrols pulled me gently as they skied behind the snowmobile. I was starting to shiver and kept passing out with the pain.

An ambulance was waiting at the top car park, where three paramedics transferred me into the vehicle. A warm blanket and a few shots of morphine for the pain and, I was starting to feel I was in safe hands. With blue lights flashing and sirens blaring, they drove me quickly to Jasper to the General Hospital. I had no memory of what happened next so Matthew continued to tell me.

When we arrived at the hospital it was very small and only had limited facilities, no CT or MRI scanners, only an x-ray machine which was mainly used for minor skiing and snowboarding injuries. As the results of my x-ray came through, they became very alarmed: it showed I had a large shadow on my chest which the doctor thought was the result of a ruptured aorta. I was now classed as critical, with a life threatening injury, and they didn't have the facilities to deal with it so they had to arrange for the Air Ambulance to fly me back to Corby to the Willow Royal Hospital. Knowing why I was in hospital, I then asked Matthew where Doug and Kathy were.

Chapter Five

Kathy was the closest to me when I had my accident. She was skiing behind me and saw me turn round and smile at her and the next minute she saw me flying through the air and landing heavily on my back. She shouted to the guys in front to stop but they had already heard my screams.

Kathy felt helpless, not knowing what she could do to help. She knew my fall was a bad one and didn't like seeing me lying in pain. She and Doug stepped back out of the way when the snow patrol arrived and watched Matthew ski with them to meet the waiting ambulance then followed behind.

Kathy was now very wobbly on her skis and the confidence she had built up was starting to fade. She couldn't wait to be back in the car park and change back into her hiking boots.

Matthew jumped in the back of the ambulance with the paramedics and threw

Doug his truck keys, telling him to drive to the hospital and meet him there. The road down from the mountain was covered in fresh snow and Doug had never driven on roads like that before. The wheels kept sliding from side to side and he had a struggle keeping the truck in a straight line, feeling like it was taking ages until they were safely on the 93A heading back into Jasper.

Jasper being a small town, the hospital was easy to find and they parked outside. Matthew was standing in the emergency entrance pacing up and down, saying they had taken me for a CT-scan to see in depth what injuries I had. They all stood together trying to stay calm while they waited for any news.

The doctor finally appeared and led them into a small room and told them I had fractured a vertebra in my lower back, saying I had completely smashed it and there was lots of loose bone around the spinal cord but that wasn't the doctor's biggest concern. He was more worried about a possible ruptured aorta and the need to get me to a hospital in Corby as soon as possible.

Doug tried to comfort Matthew but Matthew shrugged him off and took charge by giving him orders to drive back to the hotel, pack all the bags and check out then take their rented skies back to the shop and return to the hospital as soon as possible.

Back at the hotel, Kathy changed out of her salopettes and into her jeans tying her long brown hair back into a ponytail. She looked in the bathroom mirror and saw her mascara had run down her face from crying and, feeling she had to be strong for Matthew, she quickly washed her face and applied some fresh makeup then gathered their clothes and belongings together, putting them in the small overnight bag I had loaned them for the trip.

Opening the door of our room, she was amazed how different our room was to theirs. There was a huge bed that had been made without a crease in the covers and was covered with lovely pillows and cushions and there was so much space. This room was definitely an upgrade to the standard room she and Doug had and she felt quite upset that I hadn't mentioned the chance of an upgrade to her.

She found our holdall under the desk with the TV on top. There were a couple of Matthew's shirts and jeans hanging in the wardrobe along with my jeans, a pair of black trousers and a few smart sweaters and in the drawers were underwear and t-shirts, along with the swimwear we had brought to wear in the hot tub on the outside deck at the back of the hotel.

She gathered all the cosmetics and shaving bag from the bathroom, put them in the holdall with the rest and walked out of the room carrying a pair of my long boots and Matthew's shoes. She carried them to the truck where Doug was waiting for her.

After a quick stop at the ski rental shop, they were heading back to the hospital. Kathy didn't want to start crying again but, with her best friend lying in a hospital emergency room in a critical condition, she was not only worried, she was also upset that their lovely trip to Jasper had ended and she knew their holiday with us was now over. Doug steered the truck to the side of the road, stopped the engine and put his arm around Kathy and waited for her to calm down.

At the hospital they were asked to stay in the waiting room while Matthew spoke to the doctor in a private room. When they came out of the room, Matthew had tears in his eye. The doctor had explained to him that, because of the ruptured aorta, there was a medic plane already on its way to fly me as an emergency to the hospital in Corby.

Matthew had been told he had to prepare himself for me not surviving the journey as I needed emergency surgery and now would be a good time to say a goodbye as he could not go with me in the plane to the hospital as it was too small.

Poor Matthew! I just couldn't imagine how he was feeling, knowing he had well over three hours' drive back to Corby and all the time thinking I could be dead when he got there.

I looked up at Matthew from my bed and as he stopped speaking he started to cry, saying, "It was the saddest thing I had ever had to do." I felt so sorry for him, I was the one insisting we carried on skiing, I should have listened to him and stayed in the chalet until it was safe to ski down to the base of the mountain.

He said they all went to say good bye to me and found me covered in blankets, with tubes and wires attached to my body, strapped to the bed ready to be wheeled out to the medic plane when it arrived.

To help with the pain they had given me a huge amount of morphine that made me drift in and out of consciousness and I was asleep when they saw me. Kathy spoke to me first, telling me how proud she had been to have such a good friend and how she would miss me and that she would never forget me. She kissed my cheek then broke down and cried. Doug told me he would always make sure Matthew was ok and kissed me good bye.

With Kathy and Doug out of the room, Matthew said he stepped closer to the trolley where I was lying, he held my hand and found it hard to speak but finally told me to be brave, that he loved me so much and would see me in Corby. He said he couldn't say goodbye to me, he couldn't accept that that could be the last time he would see me alive.

They all watched while the paramedics wheeled the stretcher into the ambulance to take me to a field on the outskirts of Jasper, where they would meet the medic plane that was waiting for me. Nobody spoke as they watched the ambulance drive off into the distance.

They climbed into the truck with Kathy sitting in the back on her own, looking out of the window as the Jasper National Park scenery flashed past the window, thinking about how happy we all had been when we arrived, watching the elk winding in and out of the cars along the road and looking for moose.

Matthew had his eyes fixed on the road, and not a word was spoken in the three and half hour drive back to Corby. He said he seemed to be driving on auto pilot, as he was in some sort of trance all the way there.

He dropped Doug and Kathy off at our house, giving them my house and car keys and left them to fend for themselves so he could drive to the Willow Royal Hospital. Doug called the airline and arranged an early flight back to England the next morning. Their holiday was well and truly over, there was nothing they could do by staying and Matthew wanted them to leave so he could be by himself.

Driving along Park Avenue Matthew passed the shops and popular bars we would visit on a Saturday afternoon. In the summer months we would go to the Old Park Town Farmers' Market where there were locally grown vegetables, crafts, gardening plants and candy stalls. We would walk round there for ages looking for a bargain.

On a nice sunny winter's day we would park in one of the back streets and walk along the Avenue, first stopping at Café Connect, a small European Café. It didn't look much from the outside but inside it had lots of different styles of chairs and sofas all in different colours; people would be sat around low coffee tables on comfy sofas or on old-fashioned kitchen chairs around tables.

There were mirrors and large black and white pictures from the early 1900's on the walls and smaller black and white pictures of people from the same time.

A rack of European newspapers, some from the UK, were next to the long counters that displayed the tasty delights; quiches, pies, scones, yummy cakes and desserts to die for. It was a lovely warm and cosy place where friends seem to meet up. We always ordered the same thing homemade vegetable soup with homemade crusty bread. It was delicious, always reminding me of the soup my mum used to make when I was a little girl.

From there we would browse the shops going into Park Hill bookstall to find a good book and look through the cd racks. There were lots of other shops on Park Avenue. In and out of them we would go until we finally arrived at the Irish Bar called Paddy's where we would sit at our favourite table if it was free. Matthew would have his usual pint of Kilkenny and I a pint of Stella. I'm not one of those half pint kind of girls, I like my beer in a larger glass. On a Saturday afternoon they would have bands from Newfoundland, playing and singing traditional Irish music.

Today, as Matthew drove past all our favourite places, his mind was on what he was going to find when he arrived at the hospital. It was over four hours since he last saw me and he was feeling physically and emotionally tired. The question that kept going through his mind was would I still be alive.

Once through the hospital doors a young female receptionist led him to the Accident and Emergency Department where a doctor guided him into a private room that had a couple of small sofas along the wall, with a small teak wooden coffee table in the middle with a tray holding a jug of water and several glasses.

The doctor sat opposite Matthew and introduced himself as Dr Michael Tremblay an orthopaedic surgeon who specialises in thoracic and lumber spine injuries. He explained about the fracture to my L3 vertebra saying how they could not operate due to a lot of loose bone around the spinal cord. They were going to fit me with a clamshell brace and explained this device would have to be worn for several months while the fracture healed.

Matthew realised I must have survived the flight from Jasper to Corby and asked the doctor what my chances were of surviving the ruptured aorta. The doctor looked at Matthew and said the CT scan results showed the Aorta was intact and there was no rupture. Matthew, looking confused, asked Dr Tremblay if it's not a ruptured aorta, then what was the big shadow they saw on the x-ray?

Chapter Six

Matthew held my hand and moved so close to me his face was right in front of mine, I could see his eyes were full of tears as he moved even closer to kiss me.

Dr Tremblay re-entered the room and pulled a chair to the left side of my bed and sat down. He then asked me how I was feeling and had Matthew told me about what they found. I replied saying, "Yes, I believe I've broken my back." Dr Tremblay nodded saying, "Yes you have a fractured L3." The CT scan results also revealed I had a tumour on my mediastinal. This type of tumour is rare and has very few symptoms. He asked me if I was feeling unwell before my accident. I said no and asked him what the symptoms would be. You could have a cough, shortness of breath, pains in your chest, a fever, and chills, night sweats, coughing up blood, unexplained weight loss. I told him for a long time now I had been getting shortness of breath some night sweats and the occasional slight pain in my chest but nothing that would make me see a doctor. To be honest, being 41 years old, I thought I was starting to go through the change. I was having problems with heavy painful periods so I just put it all down to menopause, which I thought was something you have to put up with until it passes.

Dr Tremblay told me the date was the 2nd January year 2000. I had been in and out of consciousness for the past 5 days due to the strong drugs they had me on to help with the pain from the back injury and to keep me immobile.

He went on to say that a couple of days ago I went to theatre where I had a minor biopsy surgery. The thoracic surgeon made a small cut into my chest and collected a sample from the tumour and had it sent to the lab for testing. I looked at my chest and could see a dressing that Dr Tremblay said was covering a couple of stitches where the incision had been.

The results from the lab showed that the tumour was malignant. I heard Dr Tremblay say, "Lisa, I'm sorry the test results show you have cancer." With that, the room started to spin and I heard nothing else. I had passed out with the shock and when I came round I thought there must be some mistake; I had a fractured back, not cancer. Matthew was trying to comfort me but I felt confused and angry. Dr Tremblay told me if I hadn't had my skiing accident it's possible it would never have been detected until it was too late. He said, "I think your fractured back might just turn out to be a lucky break."

Chapter Seven

The strong drugs were making me drift in and out of sleep and my mind wandered back in time to today's date, 2nd January. This was the second time I had been given bad news on this date.

Five years previously I was taking my Christmas tree down to put it away for another year when I received a phone call from my older brother, Christian, or Chris as I've always called him. He told me that our Dad had walked into the betting shop to place a bet on a couple of horses for his afternoon TV viewing. The young man behind the counter gave him back his betting slip and, after putting it in his pocket, he turned to walk out the door then dropped to the floor before he could take another step. He was struck with a massive heart attack and when the paramedics arrived they could not revive him. My dad died that day. He was only 67 years old and the best dad I could have ever wished for. I loved him so much and still miss him terribly.

Matthew's voice interrupted my thoughts, asking me if I was ok. I shook my head and started to cry. I cried so hard I was struggling to get my breath.

Chapter Eight

Matthew had sat by my bedside every day and night since my accident. He only went home for a couple of hours to sleep, shower and change his clothes.

On New Year's Eve, the hospital was a buzz of excitement, and Matthew watched as some nurses and staff finished their shifts to go and celebrate the Millennium New Year with their loved ones and friends.

As I slept in front of Matthew, like I had done for the past few days, he looked out of the window and could see people dashing about outside, shouting, laughing and hugging each other and, apart from the nurse appearing every few hours to check my temperature and blood pressure, he saw nobody and heard from nobody.

He sat in silence until he heard the sound of fireworks as they sparked and crackled, like an explosion lighting up the midnight sky. He then knew it was midnight and bent over the bed, wished me Happy New Year and kissed my cheek, with tears running down his face as he thought that was the worst New Year's Eve he had ever had.

Chapter Nine

Mathew got home around eight thirty in the morning. There was a message from Melissa and Jessica on the answer machine that had been left in the early hours of the morning.

My beautiful daughters Melissa and Jessica didn't know about what had happened to me. We hadn't expected to hear from them until New Year's Day as they knew we were in the mountains skiing.

They must have been at a party when they left the message. He could hear music and lots of people in the background the girls were laughing as they sent us Happy New Year wishes.

Melissa, Graeme and Jessica were in England, having an amazing time. They were staying with friends and family back in their hometown of Ulverston, a small town south of the Lake District in Cumbria. This was where they grew up, where they went to school and where they were members of the local swimming club. They had so many school friends, best friends and family they had left behind when they moved to live in Canada.

They spent a day visiting their Nanna in Carlisle, making a big fuss of her and taking her out for lunch and spending hours talking about their new lives thousands of miles away. She had spoiled them back, buying them nice things from the shops they visited.

In Ulverston, the New Year's Eve party was in the Coronation Hall, which had been tastefully decorated with a huge Christmas tree at the entrance with twinkling lights, banners and balloons enhancing the rest of hall, making it very festive.

They danced the night away with their friends and, when there was only a minute until the New Year, everyone in the hall started to count the clock down until it struck twelve when alarms went off, party poppers popped, streamers were flying in the air and balloons dropped from the ceiling.

They went with their friends back to someone's house to continue the party, where Melissa and Jessica phoned us in Canada. Even though they knew we wouldn't be home, they wanted to make sure there was a message waiting for us when we arrived back from our skiing trip.

At eight thirty in the morning, Matthew picked up the phone to dial the number Melissa had rung from. With the time difference, it was three thirty in the afternoon in the UK. Julie, Melissa's friend, answered the phone and wished Matthew a Happy New Year before handing the phone over to Melissa.

Matthew had missed Melissa and Jessica's happy cheery voices even more so when he heard them shouting happy New Year down the phone. After returning the same greeting he told them what had happened to me on our skiing trip in Jasper, about the injuries to my back and that I was in the Willow Royal hospital. He did not tell them about my cancer, not wanting to worry them more than they were. They were shocked and concerned and asked Matthew to arrange an earlier flight home for them but he told them they had to stay and continue with their plans.

Chapter Ten

When Dr Tremblay thought I was ready he explained in more detail about the cancer I had. He told me I had Hodgkin's disease, which is a type of lymphoma and lymphoma is a cancer of a part of the immune system called the lymph system.

The first signs are a large mass, which was the tumour they found on my mediastinal and the disease can then spread to your nearby lymph nodes.

I asked him how I could have cancer and how did I catch it. He said, "You don't catch it and the exact cause of it is unknown. Sometimes it can just be hereditary." But there was no cancer in my family and I had no symptoms. He told me I probably had had symptoms but didn't realise, like the hot flushes I thought were the menopause. Also, I could have been having an immune reaction by having allergies.

I could recall having, on two occasions, a serious allergic reactions to aspirin and nonsteroidal anti-inflammatory drugs which I had for terrible period pains. I would have muscle cramps and intense pain in my tummy that would come in spasms. My lower back and thighs would ache not to mention the heavy bleeding.

I would buy painkillers from the chemist that were specifically for period pains. My neck and arms would go red and blotchy, making my skin itch, I'd have red eyes and my face would swell. The first time this had happened I was having coffee with my friend Linda.

I was busy ironing when she knocked on the front door. I was standing and became short of breath. Linda thought I sounded like I had asthma and became concerned. She was a nurse working in a nursing home and when she saw my rash and swollen face she didn't hesitate and rushed me to the local medical centre, where I was treated by a doctor with an adrenaline injection. The same thing happened

a couple of months later when I took some effervescent tablets for the stomach pains. The doctor prescribed me an Epipen, an adrenaline injection I could use at home if it ever happened again, and also told me to stop taking over the counter drugs for pain relief.
Looking back I wandered if these had been early symptoms of my cancer. If so, my cancer had been there for a couple of years without me knowing.

Chapter Eleven

The word "cancer" frightened me. I asked Dr Tremblay why me, what did I do wrong, what was I being punished for, have I done something crazy to cause this? The biggest question to which I wasn't sure I wanted the answer, but I had to ask, was, "Am I going to die?"

He said I was not to blame myself as it was not my fault for having cancer and not to look at ways that might somehow have prevented it.

He added that the outlook for many people diagnosed with this type of cancer is very good, that cancer does not always equal death. In most cases, cancer can be cured and Hodgkin's disease had a very good success rate.

He told me that first he was going to focus on the recovery from the fracture to my back before anything would be done about my cancer and an appointment would be set up to see an oncologist at the Kent Cancer Centre, also in Corby.

I was shocked the next day when paramedics arrived to take me to The Kent Cancer Centre. Dr Tremblay told me nothing was going to happen about my cancer until my back had healed, or at least that is what I thought he meant.

The paramedics took me to the cancer centre by ambulance and wheeled me into a large room, where they parked me in a corner. I could see more of the ceiling than anything else as I was still lying flat on my back, wearing the clamshell brace.

A man walked towards me, wearing a long white coat covering his own clothes. He was a short man of an Indian origin and introduced himself as Dr Aadi Nayar. He was very nice and said he was an oncologist who specialised in Hodgkin's disease and Non-Hodgkin's lymphoma and I would be in his care.

He had looked at the results of the biopsy that were done at the Willow Royal Hospital and explained the same as Dr Tremblay had about the type of cancer I had.

He confirmed he was happy to leave my cancer treatment until I was well on the road to recovering from my fractured back and would see me in February. This really worried me. The cancer could have killed me by then so why would they leave it so long before doing anything about it.

Dr Nayar tried to reassure me that at this stage of my cancer it was safe enough to leave it and I was not to worry about it. I was to just concentrate on getting better from my ski accident.

I couldn't get my head round it. Being told I had cancer was scary enough but being told they would not do any treatment for another month was even worse. I burst into tears when Dr Nayar gave me a card with a phone number on it so I could contact someone in cancer services if anything arose before I next saw him. He then shook my hand and left.

Chapter Twelve

Monday 10th January and Melissa, Graeme and Jessica were flying back from England. They were due to arrive at Corby airport at six o'clock in the evening. Matthew left me early afternoon so he could go shopping for groceries and get the house tidied up for them coming home.

I told Matthew I didn't want the girls and Graeme told about my cancer until the next day, I wanted them to get a good night's sleep and I would tell them in the morning when they came to visit.

I lay in the hospital bed that afternoon feeling very tired and the pain in my back was awful. To help with the pain, I had a little gadget which, when I pressed a button it would inject a controlled amount of morphine into my blood stream, making it a little more comfortable for me.

I managed to drift off into a deep sleep and was woken by a native Indian squaw looking at me. She looked to be in her early twenties. She was wearing a dress that was made from deer hide and the yoke of the dress was covered in seed beads and she had polished glass beads around her neck hanging down the front of her dress. Her black hair was parted at the top of her head and platted all the way down to her waist, tied at the bottom with some strips of rawhide. She was staring right at me and I could see she was carrying something that had a sharpened stone attached to the end of a wooden handle.

She started walking slowly towards me. I knew she was shouting at me but I couldn't hear what she was saying. I was terrified. This woman was going to kill me and I couldn't move. I needed to get away from her I needed help. I tried to scream but no sound came out of my mouth. She kept advancing towards my bed. She raised the tomahawk above her head and with one wide step she began to lower it towards my chest and I knew my end had come.

I opened my eyes, I was soaked in sweat, my heart was thumping and I looked round the room for the Indian squaw but she had gone and I realised I had been having another nightmare. Dreams like that haunted me on a regular basis while I was taking the strong pain relief drugs for my back. The dreams were always about me being in danger and being unable to get out of the hospital bed to get away.

I hated that hospital room when Matthew wasn't there, I felt lonely and scared about what was going to happen and how the cancer was going to affect my family and how everyone was going to cope with it.

Chapter Thirteen

What words was I going to use to tell the girls about my cancer? I must have rehearsed what I was going to say to them a hundred times over in my head!

Matthew said he would tell them before they came to visit me but I wanted to be the one to tell them. I knew it would upset them and I wanted to be there for them.

I glanced at the clock and knew it was time for Melissa, Graeme and Jessica to be walking through the arrivals department of the airport, looking for Matthew to take them home. Normally when they arrived back from their travels, I would be at home lighting candles and putting logs on the wood burning stove so the house would be all warm and cosy. I would make sure I had a big roast dinner waiting for them with the dining table perfectly set for a family dinner, where I would sit and listen to all their news.

The door to my room opened and Jessica walked in with Melissa, Graeme and Matthew following her, Jessica burst out crying and flung herself toward me trying her best to hug me. Matthew had not prepared them for seeing me lying immobile in bed, with tubes connected to me and me looking so pale and tired.

Melissa, being made of stronger stuff, walked up to the bed, grabbed my hand and with tears in her eyes she kissed me then said, "Hi Mum, what have you been doing on that ski slope? I thought you were a good skier!" She made me smile for the first time in days.

I made light of my skiing accident, I even joked about my new glamorous designer clamshell brace and about not having to get out of bed to go to the toilet because I had a catheter fitted. Even though they laughed I could see in their faces how concerned they were. They sympathised with poor Doug and Kathy having their holiday spoiled and I replied saying it looked like I did the same to their holiday, but they didn't comment and carried on talking about their time back in England.

They told me their Nanna was looking well and enjoying her winter indoor bowling games with her friends and that they had bumped into some of my friends. The girls told funny and interesting stories about their own friends. It was so nice to talk about something other than what was happening with me. They didn't stay long as it was getting late but I knew they would be back first thing in the morning.

I never slept that night I had more strange dreams. One of my dreams, that became a recurrent one had me running with my daughters who were around six and eight years old. We were being chased through a forest by a huge bear and every time we found a place to hide it would find us. Eventually the bear would have us trapped and, just as it was about to jump on top of us to kill us, I would wake up in a cold sweat, looking around me to see if we were safe.

Matthew brought the girls and Graeme to see me mid-morning, they were carrying bunches of lovely flowers, get well balloons and a cute little teddy bear to keep me company when I was on my own.

They were telling me they had unpacked and put the washing machine on so they would have some clean clothes. If I was at home that would have been my job, I would have also ironed everything and hung them neatly on the rail in their cupboards. They were totally spoilt.

I knew they would drag them out of the washing machine, throw them into the tumble dryer, fold them in a fashion when they were dry and Jessica would hang her clothes up in her cupboard. Melissa was the untidy one. I would put her ironing on her bed all nicely folded and the next day I would find it moved to the floor in the corner of her room so I tried not to imagine what she had done with her and Graeme's clean clothes.

I didn't want to burst their bubble but I had to tell them my other news. I took in a big breath, reached my hands out to hold Melissa and Jessica's and squeezed them tight.

Melissa looked at me and asked what was wrong. To my surprise I felt very calm and in control. I didn't waste any time and said, "I've been told I have cancer." I didn't give them chance to speak, but continued. "There's a lovely doctor I have already seen at the Kent Cancer Centre and he is going to set up some treatment for me." Jessica fell into Matthews's arms and sobbed. Graeme ran to the bathroom and vomited. Bless him, he didn't have the stomach for hospitals, let alone finding out I had cancer, and Melissa wanted answers to everything, some answers I couldn't give her.

I explained what kind of cancer I had and how it was discovered. All I could to do was reassure them that everything possible was going to be done and that I loved them all so much.

They never asked if I was going to die but I'm sure it was on their mind. They needed time to digest this terrible news. Their world had just been turned upside down and I didn't want them to go home and leave me there, I needed to be with them to protect and comfort them.

Chapter Fourteen

I felt so guilty for how much disruption and stress I was causing my family. Our lives had been ticking along quite nicely until all this happened.

Jessica was in her last year of school and finally enjoying it after making lots of new friends. When we moved to Canada, Jessica was the one that struggled the most; she was only sixteen and left all her school friends and best friends, behind including her boyfriend.

She had been looking forward to going to the Sixth Form College with her friends to do their A levels, but instead she had to start a new school and a new life in a country where she knew nobody.

She hated her new life and felt depressed all the time, she missed her boyfriend and would talk about flying back to England to live with him and his parents. I really felt sorry for her and was so worried about her.

One day Matthew and Jessica were in the garage together, Jessica was in her usual feeling sorry for herself mood, pining for her boyfriend and life back home, Matthew's patience had run out with Jessica and he wasn't going to take any more of her moaning so he offered to buy her a one way flight back to England, and told her to pack her bags and said he would drive her to the airport.

Jessica ran past me straight up the stairs and threw herself on her bed. When I walked into her room she was crying so loudly, she was gasping for breath. I was furious with Matthew. How dare he say that to her, he could be so insensitive at times and I wouldn't put up with him upsetting her.

Matthew was a very clever engineer, inventing parts for the oil industry. He was head hunted by a major oil drilling company and offered a job in Corby as a manager of a team of design engineers. He couldn't turn it down as it was putting him at the top of his career so, the afternoon after watching Princess Diana's funeral on TV, he drove round to his boss' house and told him he was leaving.

Matthew worked hard and long hours and I was proud of him but it now meant I was at home all of the time, playing mother and housewife.

We had a beautiful newly built house, it was so much bigger than our Victorian semi-detached house back in Ulverston. Our house in Corby was detached and sat at the top of a cul-de-sac, with a lovely garden that went down to the edge of a small lake.

It was on three levels with a walkout basement that had a bedroom, bathroom and a lovely living room with a small kitchen; this was where Melissa and Graeme lived. On the main floor, it was open plan with a huge glossy white kitchen with a fabulous island where I loved to bake.

On beautiful summer days, Matthew would cook dinner on the BBQ and we would all eat on the deck then Matthew and I would enjoy sitting on the garden swing with a glass of wine, watching the sun go down over the lake.

In wintertime, Matthew the girls and Graeme would clear some of the snow from the frozen lake and we would all ice skate and play ice hockey. Our lives were so different from back in England.

Chapter Fifteen

I had worked all my adult life, from the age of sixteen, starting straight after leaving school, working in an office for a wholesale pharmaceutical company. The only time I was off for any length of time was when I took maternity leave after having my two girls and back then you only got six weeks before the baby was born and six weeks after.

Matthew was my second husband. I was married in June 1978 to Steve. I had just turned twenty and he was twenty-three. When I was seventeen, my best friend Barbara set us up on a blind date. He was so handsome and seemed more mature than any of the other boys I knew. He was a police constable patrolling one of the rough areas of Carlisle. With his shift pattern and me working full time in an office, we could go for a week without seeing each other.

With his smooth talking, it didn't take him long to get his feet under the table with my mum and dad and he would be invited for Sunday dinner when he wasn't working. Then he tried his luck at playing cards with my mum and dad in the afternoon.

I used to think he was my Starsky out of the 1970's TV police series Starsky and Hutch. Falling in love with him was easy and he asked me to marry him when we were sitting on the back seat of a bus on our way home from a police dance.

We got engaged on the 3rd June 1977 and married on the same date a year later in our local village church. I had four bridesmaids and my two brothers were ushers and Steve's twin brother was his best man.

Our parents made sure it was a grand do and paid for the wedding. They had invited so many people and half of them we didn't know. I remember the day I went with my mum to buy my wedding dress. She paid £33.00 for it and I felt I looked like a princess. My dad was so proud walking me down the aisle in the church and the day flew by with a party for a hundred and fifty people in the evening.

Back in those days you had to be the first ones to leave the evening wedding party and we tried to sneak away quietly but Steve's car was trailing empty beer cans from the bumper and a four car police escort with lights flashing and sirens screeching made it a noisy exit.

Our honeymoon was two weeks in a bridal suite in a luxury hotel in Bournemouth - the first time we had slept all night in a bed together as our parents had very strict rules about sleeping together out of wedlock.

We wanted children right away while we were still young so we wouldn't be too old to enjoy our lives when they had flown the nest. Melissa was born in September 1979 and Jessica in February 1982.

We had very little money but we made the most out of what we had and like a lot of young families, everything revolved around the children.

We couldn't go to the pubs or go dancing in the disco like we did before the girls were born so our nights out were at friends' houses where we would take the girls with us and tuck them up in our friend's bed. They were fun times, playing Trivial Pursuit and drinking too much Cinzano cocktails.

With me still working full time we would save hard all year and book the cheapest holiday to Spain and go with our best friends and their children.

Steve was promoted to Police Sergeant and we moved to Ulverston in 1986.

As the girls grew up and were in high school, Steve and I had more time to do things together, but instead he took up squash and golf and I joined the local running club. Over time, we drifted apart and, when we did have nights out together, it would always end in us arguing.

We became insecure and would accuse each other of cheating. The front door would slam as one of us stormed out of the house after another argument. I don't think I realised how unhappy I was until my dad died.

Mum and dad came to stay with us for Christmas 1994 and on Christmas Eve my dad took me for our father-daughter drink. He always liked to have me to himself for a couple of hours.

My dad never interfered in my life but he could feel the atmosphere in the house and could see Steve and I weren't getting on so he asked me if everything was alright between us. I always kept my problems to myself and told him we were fine. The words he said next never meant anything to me until he died a week later. He said, "Lisa, you only get one life and that can be too short. You're a beautiful woman inside and out and, if you're not happy, then change it, and if you can't change it then fix it."

I thought seriously about whether my marriage was worth fixing and I didn't think it was. I had not been happy for a long time so I ended our marriage a month later and we were divorced in June 1995, just after what would have been our seventeenth wedding anniversary, and I met Matthew eight months later.

Chapter Sixteen

One Saturday night when I was in our local pub with my friend Linda I saw him looking at me from across the bar, I didn't really pay much attention to it but Linda kept going on about it. She was always trying to fix me up with men in the pub. He eventually came over and offered to buy me a drink, I refused. I wasn't ready for another man in my life.

I was working as a receptionist in one of the optician's and the next day Matthew walked up to my desk and asked me if I would go for dinner with him the next night. Linda was really in my bad books for telling Matthew where I worked.

I had been in my teens the last time I went on a date so I found it a bit scary. I wore the only dress I owned, a plain black one that was fitted and had thin shoulder straps. Matthew took me to a very classy restaurant a short drive out of Ulverston. He had reserved a cosy table next to the window and ordered a bottle of champagne. We had a beautiful meal and, with plenty of conversation, he had me interested in him. We saw a lot of each other after that date, going for mid-week drinks in the local pub and for dinner on a Saturday night then on a Sunday, if the weather was good, he would pick me up on his motorbike and he'd drive us to the Lake District stopping off for lunch in Windermere.

I had bought a lovely little house after my divorce from Steve and I lived there with Melissa and Jessica. Matthew lived in a small village just outside Ulverston and ended up moving in with us. In February 1996, Matthew and I bought a lovely Victorian semi-detached house and turned it into a home for the four of us.

The girls adored Matthew and he enjoyed living with us as a family so, on Christmas Day, I asked him to marry me. I had written 'marry me' on a card and tied it on a bottle of champagne that I had wrapped up and given to him as a Christmas present.

We were married in May 1997, not the big flash wedding like I had when I married Steve. There were only thirty people at our wedding when we were married in the council chambers in Ulverston. I had designed my own wedding dress and had it made for me and it cost a lot more than £33.00. We had our reception in the local hall and Melissa's friend sang for us.

Matthew was Scottish and looked very smart in his kilt and he was thrilled when he heard a traditional Scottish piper play the "Flower of Scotland" as we walked out of the council chambers.

Our honeymoon was no sexy affair. It was in the Isle of Man, marshalling the TT Races, sharing a room with four of our biker friends in a small hotel.

We had a good life together and were very settled. I had a good routine juggling work, family and fun. I had lots of good friends. I still did my running, but not to the extent I did when I was married to Steve. It was a long time since I had been this happy.

I never expected Matthew to come home one day and say he wanted to accept a job he had been offered in Canada and move us thousands of miles away. I was not sure this was what I wanted but I was Matthew's wife and I would never stand in his way.

Matthew left for Canada four months after we were married. Melissa and Jessica were in their last year of school and sixth form college so we didn't leave until the following July.

Nine months Matthew and I were apart and I was living in a rented furnished house with the girls after I had sold our lovely house and packed everything up to be shipped over to Canada.

Apart from Matthew not being around, life didn't change that much for me. I still went to work as a receptionist at the local doctor's surgery. The girls went to school and college and I still had Linda coming round for coffee and I would meet my friends in the pub at the weekend.

I missed Matthew but was enjoying my life and, the closer it got to the big day for us to leave the more I was getting cold feet. The night before we left, our friends threw a big farewell party in our local pub and I stood crying in the ladies toilets, telling my best friend I didn't want to go.

Chapter Seventeen

Things were different for me now. For the first time in my life, I wasn't going out to work, which meant I was always around for Matthew and the girls. I was the one who made sure everything in the house ran smoothly and spent days doing housework and cooking. It was a novelty at first with us enjoying all the new experiences Canada had to offer.

How my life was going to change! I wished I'd never been told I had cancer. I wished I had never insisted on going skiing.

Matthew was going back to work for a couple of hours today so in the morning he came to visit me by himself. He told me Melissa, Jessica and Graeme were struggling with the news of my cancer and he didn't know what to do as he was trying to come to terms with it himself.

This was not the time for me to be apart from them, my family needed me so I pressed the bell for the nurse and when she arrived I told her I needed to speak to the doctor. Dr Tremblay came into my room an hour later and I told him it was impossible for me to stay in hospital, I was needed at home. Matthew wasn't happy with my decision and said I was being stupid. He didn't know how I was going to manage at home. Managing at home was the last thing on my mind, I had always been there for my girls and I wasn't about to stop now.

Dr Tremblay was not very happy either and reminded me I had a broken back and needed to be immobile for another couple of weeks before I could attempt getting out of bed. I told him I didn't care about me and to arrange for my discharge.

Matthew was angry and told me he wouldn't be able to take care of me at home and insisted I stay where I was. I didn't care what Matthew thought I just wanted go home. Later that day, after everything was set up, the nurse disconnected me from the saline drip and morphine pump then removed the cannula from my hand. I was given a bag of prescription drugs that included bottles of anti-sickness and morphine tablets.

Chapter Eighteen

The Ambulance crew arrived and transferred me onto their trolley and wheeled me out of the hospital and into the ambulance. Driving me home was the easy part for the crew. Getting me upstairs to bed was another matter, especially with Matthew huffing and puffing behind them.

When the crew left after tucking me up into bed Matthew and the girls stood around the bed not sure what to do next. Matthew was in a foul mood. He shook his head at me then walked off down the stairs. The girls and Graeme were pleased to see me even though they thought I was crazy for discharging myself. They knew Matthew wasn't happy about me being at home but they were going to make sure I was looked after and started to fuss over me, giving me magazines, a new book to read and a new CD to listen to.

They switched the TV on so I could watch my favourite programme, The Oprah Winfrey Show. I could be busy all day in the house but would always sit on the sofa with a cup of coffee in time for the start of the show. It did feel good to be home and in my own bed.

Jessica told me she didn't like seeing me in the hospital and hated being in the house without me. Melissa being the practical one, was more concerned about how I was going to get to the toilet. I explained I was catheterized and Matthew would have to empty the bag for me and that the district nurse would call each day to check all was well. Melissa wasn't going to have Matthew do that, she said it would be her job. After the girls finished welcoming me home Matthew came upstairs to apologise for his behaviour. Poor Matthew! I did feel sorry for him he was well out of his comfort zone. He had never seen me ill before other than a bout of bad period pains and even then I would put on a brave face.

Things were about to change. I was the one who did everything in the house and now it was down to them to pull together and share the housework and cooking. I told Matthew maybe he needed to organise a routine with the girls. I told him Melissa would help me with any hygiene needs, which would be good patient care experience for her and told him to keep an eye on Jessica but not to boss her about.

Coming home had exhausted me and sleep came quickly when I was finally left on my own. When I woke up I was in so much pain as the shot of morphine they gave me before I left the hospital was starting to wear off. I no longer had a bell I could press for the nurses to come running and I knew shouting for Matthew was a waste of breath as he wouldn't hear me. I was in agony. The pain was making me feel sick.

Jessica was a welcome sight as she popped her head round the bedroom door and, after I explained which tablets and how many I needed, she popped them into my mouth then sat on the bed holding my hand waiting for the pain to ease.

Jessica got really upset. She hadn't realised I would be in so much pain and I realised she was going to find all this hard to cope with. I arranged with all three of them to make sure someone checked on me regularly. If I was to be alone upstairs for any length of time then I wouldn't end up in that state again.

After a few days I could see why they didn't want me to leave the hospital. The amount of morphine I had been having intravenously had totally controlled my pain. Now the pain was unbearable and I was only taking painkillers when I couldn't stand the pain which meant I was chasing the pain instead of managing it.

Dr Tremblay told me I had to stay in bed for four weeks I had no idea how I was going to manage that when everything was starting to get on my nerves.

I became miserable and depressed and poor Matthew would get the brunt of it. I would hear raised voices as Matthew and Jessica would clash over something and I would blame Matthew for not being nice to her where, in reality, she had probably done or said something wrong.

I'd accuse him of not making the dinner properly, leaving the house untidy, and his clothes lying around the bedroom, not leaving the bathroom clean...... In my eyes, he couldn't do anything right.

Matthew would storm out of the bedroom and leave me to think about how horrible I was being to him. Our bedroom had gone from being full of passion to a battlefield and I was the one starting every battle. Normally Matthew and I never fell out. We would have disagreements but not real rows. Matthew wasn't the argumentative type and now I was pushing all his buttons. I don't know how I could be such a bitch as it was not like me.

Matthew's boss allowed him to work from home and he would shut himself in his office for hours and not speak to any of us. This would drive me mad. He was supposed to be looking after me, not ignoring me.

I told Melissa one day that I felt like a lion that was locked in a small cage and needed desperately to get out. I think the girls were glad to be back at school and college and Graeme back at work.

Melissa always made sure I was ok before she went to college. She would wash me, removing the clamshell brace while I lay flat on the bed and sponge down my body. She even shaved my legs and rubbed body cream on them and my arms, making me feel clean and fresh. At first it felt strange and embarrassing, my daughter taking care of my hygiene needs but I had no choice and it didn't seem to bother her.

After four painful weeks, I was able to get out of bed with someone helping me. I still had to wear the brace and I was not allowed to twist from side to side or try to bend.

With Matthews's help the first thing I did was slowly walk to the bedroom window and look out. It was -30c outside, everything was covered with snow and it glistened in the bright sunshine.

The spruce trees at the bottom of the garden looked so pretty with their branches hanging heavy with the snow. I could see where Graeme and the girls had dug a pathway in the snow to walk down to the frozen lake and they had cleared an area of the lake to ice skate on. When I was in bed, I would hear them outside having fun but could never see them until now.

I was able to walk around the bedroom but walking down stairs had to wait another couple of days. Having my first shower was a real task but, with Melissa's help, I managed to step under the warm running water and could feel it cascading over my head and face. My long hair hadn't been washed properly since the day of my accident and it felt good to fluff it up with bubbles from the shampoo.

The clamshell brace I was wearing was perforated with holes and the water was running down the inside from the top and pouring out through the holes. It did look quite comical but it would have been nice to stand there totally naked and have a proper shower.

Jessica came into the bedroom to join us and she pampered me by first styling my hair then painting a lovely deep red colour onto my finger and toenails. By the time I had put some make up on and sprayed myself with perfume I was starting to look like my old self, that's if you looked beyond the clamshell brace.

I attended the Orthopaedic clinic every two weeks and Dr Tremblay would show me the x-ray results of how my body was growing a new vertebra. It was fascinating to see after each x-ray that a bit more had grown. It's amazing how your body heals itself.

Chapter Nineteen

Physiotherapy started in the middle of February and I would go twice a week.
My physiotherapist, who was called Ryan, was excellent at his job and pretty nice on the eye with his blonde hair and strong, broad body. At first he gave me gentle exercises, hands on my hips and slow steps to the left then the same to the right. He would have me using small hand weights where I would have to reach forward at shoulder level then pull back. A few weeks later I advanced to another couple of exercises and they were really hard and painful to do. At home I would follow the exercise programme Ryan set up for me, doing my best to get myself back to normal.

It had been six tough weeks since my life changed after my accident on the ski slopes. I knew it would be a slow recovery and, with my cancer to deal with, I knew I had a long journey ahead of me.

It was still very cold outside, with the temperature around -20c. The house was always lovely and warm because Matthew would make sure the fire was stacked with logs before he went to work. I found putting logs on the fire a major task. Actually, there wasn't much I could do other than sit on the sofa and watch a bit of TV or read my book, all pretty boring for someone who had been so active.

I felt my cancer had been put to the back of everyone's mind. When I would bring it up in conversation Matthew never wanted to discuss it and kept telling me to just concentrate on getting my back better.

We had stopped arguing over things and Matthew would bury his head in his work, he would come home, eat his dinner then sit in his office for the rest of the night. I just let him get on with it. I guess it was his way of dealing with everything. There were days when I would sit alone in the afternoon, crying with worry about the future and in need of being wrapped in Matthew's arms, with him reassuring me everything would be ok. By the time everyone arrived home I would put my happy face on and be upbeat, asking them all about their day and not one of them ever knew how alone and upset. I had been, I just tried my best to keep things as normal as possible.

Chapter Twenty

A letter arrived in the mail for me for an appointment to see Dr Nayar at the Kent Cancer Centre in two weeks, on Monday 6th March at 10.30am. I must have read it ten times over. The letter sat on the kitchen counter in front of my novelty mail holder with two little chickens on the front and, every time I looked over, it would draw me to it and I would keep picking it up to read it.

I had no idea what was going to happen next. I couldn't remember what they had originally told me about my cancer, everything was now such a blur. I was becoming concerned as to how much the cancer had grown since my accident and I felt like I was sitting on a ticking time bomb that was due to go off any day.

When my phone rang, I answered it right away, I could hear the familiar voice of my mum asking me how I was feeling. Matthew had phoned her a couple of days after my skiing accident and told her about my broken back and, after the girls had returned and I was back home, I called her to tell her about my diagnosis of cancer.

My mum was 67 years old and had lived on her own for five years since my dad died. Dad was only 53 when he had his first heart attack and had to retire from his job as an Air Ministry Police Constable, he realised he was on borrowed time and sold the country family home we all grew up in. They bought a nice two-bedroom apartment in a lovely cul de sac within easy reach of the city centre. The apartments were in blocks of four, two apartments at the top and two at the bottom, mum and dad had one of the top ones feeling they were more secure.

Mum was very much against dad's idea to move; she wanted to stay in the house where she had raised her family. Our bedrooms had stayed the same even though we had all moved out years ago. Mine and my brother's children would now occupy our old rooms and sleep in our old beds when they were having sleepovers at weekends with their Nanna and Granddad.

The apartments were all new and built for the over fifties and it didn't take long for mum and dad to make new friends with the neighbours and settle into enjoying their new home and lifestyle. After dad died, it was those friends who were always there for mum and, with my two brothers living close by, it made it a bit easier for her when we packed up and moved to Canada.

I found it hard telling mum my news, I expected her to say caring words to make me feel better but she just broke down and cried. I guess she didn't really know what to say, she was nearly four thousand miles away and I had never been seriously ill before. Neither had my brothers. Mum never expected any of her children even as adults, to get an illness that could lead to them dying. She told me she would fly over and be with me and help me around the house but I was flat on my back in bed and Matthew and I were at each other's throats and we needed to get our heads round everything that had happened and get into some kind of routine. I knew that as much as I would love mum to be with me, it wouldn't work so I told her she could come when I was out of the clamshell brace and before my cancer treatment. Poor mum was worried sick and she would phone me every day at eight thirty in the morning, which was three thirty in the afternoon her time.

On the day of my appointment, Matthew took time off work to take me and I was feeling really nervous. Getting into Matthew's truck was a struggle. It was much higher than Melissa's car and I was still wearing my clamshell brace and still having pain spasms in my back.

The waiting room was full of people, some young, some old, some with fine patchy hair and some bald. There was a pretty woman with a colourful bandana around her head, obviously hiding a head with no hair. Matthew wasn't feeling very comfortable being in this place. He kept fidgeting in his seat and neither of us spoke while we sat and waited for my turn to see the doctor.

When the nurse called my name we walked into a small room that was well lit, even though it had no windows. Dr Nayar stood up from behind his desk, wearing a long white coat that covered his clothes. He walked over to us and shuck our hands, guiding us to two seats where we sat down. He asked me how I was feeling and if my back was recovering but I couldn't answer him, I just sat there staring at him and I was glad when Matthew spoke for me. I didn't mean to be ignorant. I was just so nervous.

He said most patients don't take everything in the first time they are told they have cancer so he explained again, repeating what he had told me in January. He said he had arranged for me to have another biopsy, this time a needle biopsy, so they could take another sample from the tumour.

Lying flat on the treatment bed with Matthew holding my hand Dr Nayar removed the front of my brace and cleaned an area on my chest, numbed the area with some medication then inserted a needle through my chest and into the tumour to take the sample. I could see what he was doing and I was very tense but I didn't feel a thing. He also took a couple of vials of blood and sent them all off to the lab for testing.

I couldn't understand why they were doing all these tests when they already had results from the sample they had taken from the tumour a couple of days after my skiing accident.

After I was dressed and safely back into my brace, he told me they wanted to redo the biopsy and take their own sample so they could double check everything.

I wanted to know what treatment I was going to have and when would it start and he told me I would start chemotherapy the following week as he didn't expect the results of my biopsy to be any different from the first one. Matthew drove us back home and I broke the news to the girls about my chemotherapy.

Why can't I be normal? Why am I the one to break my back in a skiing accident and now have to go through chemotherapy? Why can't I be normal and have just one thing wrong with me at a time? I had never seen anyone go through chemotherapy before so I didn't know what to expect. My head was in such a spin, I needed to get out of the house and do something normal to try and forget about everything else.

Melissa and Jessica took me to the shopping mall to cheer me up and it did the trick. I had a lovely day walking from shop to shop even though I had to keep stopping at intervals to rest. We sat and watched the dolphin show then we watched the elderly people skating on the ice rink. Round and round they went, holding hands. I don't think the girls realised how much of a tonic it was for me that day.

Chapter Twenty One

Monday morning and I was ready for my appointment at the Kent Cancer Centre for the start of my chemotherapy. I couldn't sleep the night before, I was feeling nervous, anxious and tired.

Matthew and I sat in a small waiting room just outside the chemotherapy unit. The doors were open and I could see nurses attending to patients sitting in chairs, and wondered which chair I would be sitting in. A nurse came out and asked if I had an appointment and I told her I had to see Dr Nayar first. She was ever so nice and friendly and I hoped she would be the nurse who would be attending to me.

Matthew, being very supportive, held my hand as we walked into Dr Nayar's treatment room. Dr Nayar was smiling and told me he had some good news for me, that I would not be having chemotherapy that day or any other day and that he did not think I had cancer. I looked at Matthew then back to Dr Nayar my heart beating so fast I thought it was going to come out of my chest. My hands were shaking and I started to cry. Matthew hugged me, I think more in relief than to comfort me.

Dr Nayar explained the test results for the needle biopsy came back with no trace of cancer cells and my blood count was normal. I was stunned. I didn't know what to say. Matthew's face was lit up, he was so happy. He kept thanking Dr Nayar.

I was confused and asked Dr Nayar how, if I didn't have cancer, I had a tumour inside my chest. I had seen the x-ray result and the tumour wasn't small; it looked like the size of a small lemon. He told me it was possibly a growth that I had had all my life and it was nothing to worry about.

He explained that Instead of cancer cells in the biopsy sample, they found I had traces of something called Systemic Mast Cell Disease. Matthew and I had never heard of it so he explained that mast cells are produced in the bone marrow, are an important part of the immune system and fight infection. The cells can trigger an allergic reaction as they release histamine and other chemicals into the blood stream. Histamine makes blood vessels expand and the surrounding skin becomes red, itchy and swollen. They can create a build-up of mucus in the airways, which become narrower and this is known as an allergic reaction, increasing the risk of an anaphylaxis shock. The cause of mast cell disease is unknown but something called genetic mutation makes the mast cells more sensitive to the effects of a type of protein called stem cell factor. When the bone marrow is exposed to stem cell factor, it produces more mast cells than the body can cope with which leads to allergic reactions. So the same allergic reactions I had been getting were not linked to cancer but to mast cell disease and the only treatment for mast cell disease was daily antihistamines. Dr Nayar handed me a prescription for some antihistamines and told me had no other concerns about my health.

Chapter Twenty Two

I walked out of Dr Nayar's treatment room in a daze. Matthew grabbed my hand and lifted it up to his lips and kissed my fingers. He told me he loved me and how pleased he was that my cancer scare was over and all I had to do now was wait a couple of weeks for the clamshell brace to come off and life could start to get back to normal.

We couldn't wait to get home and tell the girls and Graeme. They would be so pleased so, on the way home, Matthew drove to the liquor store and bought a couple of bottles of Veuve Clicquot champagne and said, "Tonight we celebrate." There was no one home when we got back so by the time the girls and Graeme walked in the house, I had party food laid out on the kitchen island with five champagne flutes waiting to be filled.

I was bursting to tell them my news and blurted it out as soon as I saw them Matthew popped the cork from one of the bottles of bubbly and poured it into the glasses. We all cried, laughed and hugged each other. Melissa said, "We couldn't have a party without music," and put a cd into the music system and with Matthew in the middle of Melissa and Jessica, they all danced and sang along to the songs, waving their arms in the air.

We had a lovely night and the girls played DJ putting on one song after another and dancing around the room. It seemed a long time since we had all laughed as much as we did that night.

After the girls and Graeme had gone to bed, Matthew sat curled up to me on the sofa and we started making plans for the future. Matthew told me he had seen a two acre piece of land for sale which he was interested in buying. Feeling so relieved that we could now focus on something positive, the next morning we drove west out of Corby and into the countryside to check it out.

The land was thick with trees some spruce and some poplar, and the Saskatchewan River ran past the land, about five hundred yards down a shallow bank. It was a beautiful area and a perfect piece of land to build a house on. Matthew said he wanted to design us a house and that he had already drawn up some ideas so he phoned the Real Estate agent and put in an offer in for the land, which was accepted the next morning.

Our house went up for sale and everything became very busy. The realtor would call with a time he wanted to show potential buyers round and we would go to Tim Horton's and have coffee while we waited for them to leave.

Our house sold fast and the new buyers wanted in within six weeks so we had to find somewhere to live. We needed to rent an apartment while the house was being built and we found one on the sixteenth floor of a tall tower block next to the river that over looked the city.

Matthew had arranged to interview a builder as a project manager to oversee the building of our new house and everything was ready to start as soon as we completed with the new buyers on our house.

It had been a stressful couple of weeks but we were excited. We now felt we had our lives back and nothing was going to get in the way of us having our dream home in the country. It was just what we needed after three months of worry.

Chapter Twenty Three

I had spent hours on the phone to family and friends spreading the good news about not having cancer and our plans for our new house. Everyone was so happy and pleased for us and, by the time I made the last call, I was exhausted.

I only had a couple of weeks left wearing the clamshell brace and had an appointment to see Dr Tremblay the next day. Melissa drove me to the Willow Royal Hospital for my appointment and, for once, we were in high spirits.

I liked Dr Tremblay. He was always cheerful and chatty. He sent me for an x-ray so he could see how my back was progressing and the results showed everything was healing nicely. He was so pleased and told me my brace could come off at the next appointment in two weeks.

As I was about to leave he asked me if I was feeling ok. He said I looked very pale and tired. I told him about the busy couple of weeks with the sale of our house and our plans for the new one. He thought I was taking too much on with my cancer treatment just ahead of me. I told him the good news and he was shocked and asked me to sit back down and tell him exactly what Dr Nayar had told me.

He said he couldn't understand why Dr Nayar had said that because the biopsy results they had taken just after my accident definitely showed I had Hodgkin's disease, and advised me to make another appointment to see Dr Nayar to discuss it further.

Melissa and I left the Willow Royal Hospital with a very uneasy feeling. I phoned the Kent Cancer Centre as soon as we got home and made an urgent appointment for the next day to see Dr Nayar. Again Dr Nayar assured me I did not have cancer I had Mast Cell Disease.

A couple of days had passed since seeing Dr Nayar again and something started nagging away inside my head. I kept going from being happy to being afraid. Something was trying to tell me something was wrong. I had a burning sensation in my gut and it wouldn't go away. I kept telling myself to ignore it but I couldn't. I started to question what Dr Nayar had said and Dr Tremblay's concern was becoming more important.

I phoned Matthew at his work and told him something was wrong. He was not very happy with me and told me I was being stupid, that there was no way the oncologist would get anything wrong. He told me to focus on our new house and to be more positive about our future. I could feel myself starting to cry but I knew Matthew didn't want to talk about it so I changed the subject and told him I would see him at suppertime.

Matthew never mentioned my phone call when he came home and I knew he didn't want me to bring the subject up again. Everybody was so happy and Matthew wanted no more talk about cancer.

For days these feelings haunted me. I tried to put them out of my mind but they wouldn't go away. I knew I had to make Matthew listen to me I was sure something was seriously wrong and I wasn't going to rest until I got to the bottom of it.

I called Dr Tremblay's secretary at the Willow Royal and asked if she could get Dr Tremblay to call me and when I received his call an hour later, I told him about my second appointment with Dr Nayar and how Matthew had reacted when I told him of my concerns. Dr Tremblay told me not to ignore my gut feelings and to get a second opinion as he was sure the oncologist was wrong.

That evening, Melissa and Graeme had gone for an early pizza then on to the movies and Jessica had gone to her friends after school so we had the house to ourselves. I made a special supper for Matthew and me and had the table looking nice when he came home from work. I needed to tell him how I was feeling and sitting round the table eating with a nice glass of wine was where I got the best of his attention.

After a lengthy discussion, he still didn't think the oncologist was wrong but said he would support me if I really felt I needed a second opinion. I phoned to make another appointment to see Dr Nayar at the Kent Cancer Centre and when Matthew and I walked into his treatment room he was confused about why we needed to see him so urgently. Matthew explained our concerns to him and that we wanted to have a second opinion. I could see from Dr Nayar's face that he wasn't very happy with us. He told us we were wasting our time, that I didn't have cancer, and I should accept it. He said I could go back to see him in six months for a further check-up if it would make me feel better but I was straight with him and told him I had no confidence in his diagnosis. He said that when we had found another oncologist for a second opinion, his secretary would forward my medical notes but he never offered any advice as to which oncologist to go to. It was a very stressful appointment and we were now on our own to find the right doctor to help us.

That appointment upset me for days. I thought Dr Nayar would have automatically recommended another oncologist for me to see but he didn't and even though Matthew supported me I wasn't sure he believed I was doing the right thing.

I had no idea where to start to look for another oncologist and without Matthew's help I wouldn't have got any further. Matthew sat at his computer every night after supper researching where best to get a second opinion, finally telling me he thought the best place to go was the Weston Clinic in Phoenix Arizona, miles away in America. Could he not find anywhere closer in Canada?

Matthew said if we were to get a second opinion he wanted it to be from one of the best oncologists he could find and he felt the Weston Clinic could offer that.

The next day he phoned the Weston Clinic and made an appointment for me to see someone in a couple of weeks' time. My next appointment with Dr Tremblay was a few days before we were due to fly out to Phoenix.

Another x-ray gave good results and my clamshell brace was removed. After wearing it for four months it now felt very strange without it. Dr Tremblay was very pleased to hear about the appointment we had set up at the Weston Clinic and wished me a safe trip.

Chapter Twenty Four

On Saturday 8th April, Matthew and I flew out of Corby International Airport for Phoenix Arizona. I had never been to America before and wished this was a nice holiday we were going on, not a trip to a clinic.

The flight was only three and half hours and we were soon landing in Phoenix Sky Harbour International Airport. As they opened the aeroplane doors to disembark, the heat was unbelievable, the pilot had said on landing that it was +33c. When we left Corby there was snow on the ground and it was cold with a temperature of -5c.

We picked up a hire car and drove through the city that had large cactus plants and palm trees lining the streets. It was very impressive with lots of different coloured flowers everywhere.

Phoenix, the capital city of Arizona, is flat, apart from the mountains around it. The

Weston Clinic was on the edge of the city and The Lizard Hotel we were booked into was only walking distance from the clinic.

We checked in and were shown to a lovely room on the ground floor with doors that opened on to a private patio in front of the hotel swimming pool that looked inviting, but as it was late afternoon we changed into some cooler clothes and went for a walk.

Further down the road a new residential subdivision was being built so we went into the show home to have a look round. We were obsessed with new houses, now that we were planning to build our own.

A very smart sales lady who looked like she had walked off the catwalk with her tightly fitted red dress and high heels greeted us at the door. We had to pretend we were potential buyers otherwise, we wouldn't have been allowed in.

She showed us into a little office that had been set up in part of the garage. She showed us a map on the wall where building lots of four acres were set out for each house to be built on and explained how she would help us design a home to our own specification and showed us some custom plans of different styles of house. The houses being built were to be in the price region of three million dollars and above. It was to be a guarded, gated community. She explained how close the nearest school was and about the walking trails lined with cactus.

Entering the house, we removed our shoes and the sales lady shrunk five inches after she removed hers.

It was a stunning house and we left with a brochure full of information and the sales lady's business card. It sure gave us an insight in how the wealthy live.

Sunset was around seven o'clock and we had heard it was a sight not to be missed so we walked a little way across the cracked, dry, dusty surface of the dessert, watching where we walked so we didn't step on a lizard or any other creature. We were excited to see a small dust devil travelling at speed in front of us.

The sun was dropping behind the desert mountains and in the distance, the sky was purple with vibrant red and orange strips where it met the land, covering the desert sand in purple, with every plant shining as if lamps lit them up. It was such a beautiful and amazing sight to see.

The next morning we went to Arizona Mills, a huge shopping mall with a massive IMAX theatre, a sea life aquarium and a fabulous rainforest café. It was a more comfortable temperature in there and nice to get out of the heat from outside.

We loved walking round, wandering in and out of the shops. We found the clothes were cheaper than they were back in Canada and we bought a couple of items.

We left there and called into the Scottsdale Fashion Mall, which offered the best brands for exclusive shoppers such as Armani, Dillard's, Gucci and Jimmy Choo and, after checking a few price tags, we left knowing everything was well out of our price range. We returned to the hotel and had a relaxing afternoon sitting around the swimming pool.

Chapter Twenty Five

Matthew and I had a lovely weekend, just what we needed after our long spell of stress since my accident. Apart from a bit of back pain I was feeling quite well and looked good with the bit of colour I had on my skin from our couple of days in the sun.

My appointment at the Weston Clinic was booked for ten o'clock and the night before I couldn't get to sleep, knowing our weekend was only a stopgap, as the stress and worry of cancer was at the front of my mind again.

I woke before Matthew and trying not to wake him, I sat at the little desk in the corner and switched on the lamp. I wanted to be prepared for my appointment, to make sure I wrote down everything Dr Nayar had originally said about being diagnosed with Hodgkin's disease and Mast Cell disease.

I wrote all the symptoms I believed I had, starting right back to my allergic reactions to the period pain tablets I had taken when I was still living in the UK. I racked my brain for knowledge of any family history of cancer but the only people in our family that I knew had died of cancer were my grandfathers; one died of leukaemia and the other of lung cancer but that was years ago when I was a young girl.

My grandmothers both died of a heart attack so there was no cancer there. My mum was one of six children, having two brothers and three sisters. One sister died when she was young but that wasn't from cancer either.

My dad was one of five, he had two brothers and two sisters and none of them had died of cancer. Heart failure seemed to be the thing that ran through his family.

I had many questions in my head to which I wanted answers and I started right at the beginning and listed them so I wouldn't forget to ask anything important.

If I did have cancer, I wanted them to confirm what type and what stage it was at.

I wanted to have any pathology reports explained clearly to me and wanted to ask if I could have copies.

If my cancer is re-diagnosed what treatment options would be available to me?

What would the benefits of the treatment be?

What would the side effects of each treatment be?

Was one treatment better than another?

How would they know the treatment would help me?

Would I be treated in the Weston Clinic or back home in Corby?

Could they give me any brochures or printed information leaflets that I could take with me?

What would the tests and treatment be?

I put the list to one side, made a cup of coffee for Matthew and crawled back into bed and we both sat chatting while drinking our hot drinks.

It was only a short walk to the Weston Clinic and the sun was beating down from the sky. The hotel receptionist told us it was already

+3c so I was glad I was wearing a thin summer dress.

Entering the clinic there was a reception desk to the right with three girls ready to greet us. They were wearing smart blue uniforms - skirt, jacket and crisp white shirts with a coloured scarf tied around their necks and they looked more like air hostesses than receptionists. Matthew explained why we were there and we were asked to sit in the waiting area that was set in a half circle with six or seven rows deep. It looked a very busy place with a lot of patients waiting to be seen.

We were early for our appointment and sat for about half an hour before being called. I was starting to feel cold. The air-conditioning was set so low that, in my thin summer dress, I felt like I was sitting in a fridge.

My name was called by the receptionist and we were directed to a room that was more like an office than a treatment room, with the name Dr Nathan A Warwick on the door.

Dr Warwick looked more like a businessman than a doctor. He was very handsome, about late thirties, with thick dark brown hair that had been pushed back from his face with gel. He was wearing a very smart, expensive looking dark grey suit with a light grey and white striped shirt, a light grey tie that was held together by a silver tie clip engraved with his initials and his black shoes were shining like a mirror.

He welcomed us to the Weston Clinic and introduced himself as a Haematologist – Oncologist specialising in the diagnosis, treatment and prevention of blood diseases and cancers such haemophilia, sickle-cell, Hodgkin's, non-Hodgkin's lymphoma, leukaemia and myeloma.

He told us we could call him Nathan instead of Dr Warwick and asked how our flight over had been and what the weather was like back at home in Corby. Matthew once again took the lead and explained the reasons why we needed a second opinion and about losing confidence in Dr Nayar.

Nathan explained he had received my medical details from the Kent Cancer Centre and he had set up a program with appointments that would be spread over the next few days for me to undergo various tests. I told him I had a list of questions I needed answered and he said I was to keep them until all the tests had been done.

My first appointment was at one o'clock that afternoon and, before returning to the hotel for lunch, we had to go to their finance office to be registered and they took down all my details including our bank account numbers.

We returned to the clinic at one o'clock and again we had to sit with the circle of patients waiting to be called for appointments. This time I went prepared and took a cardigan with me so I wouldn't be cold.

I was shown to a changing room along the right side of the waiting area and given a hospital gown and dressing coat to change into, placing my own clothes in a locker. I then entered a treatment room where Nathan and a nurse were waiting for me. He introduced the nurse as Sister Megan King, a lovely lady in her mid-forties.

Megan was going to be present in every appointment they had set up for me and that afternoon I was to have a physical examination and blood tests Megan took my height and weight then asked me to lie on the treatment bed where she covered me over with a light blanket.

She took my blood pressure and attached a pulse oximeter to the index finger on my right hand, explaining this was to assess my breathing to measure my heart rate. Nathan examined my neck, armpits and each side of my groin, feeling for any lumps or anything that didn't feel normal.

The nurse then inserted a needle into a vein on the back of my left hand and attached a cannula to it. She took several vials of blood and Nathan explained he wanted a full blood count to check my red and white blood cells, haemoglobin, hematocrit, and platelets. My appointment was over and I was to return the next day again at one o'clock as I was booked in for a bone density scan.

Matthew was not happy as he felt they could have done more tests that day. After all, we were only here for a couple of days. The bone density scan was pretty straight forward, done in the radiology department in the clinic where Megan was waiting to meet me. She gave me various forms to fill in and sign, mainly about medication and calcium supplement or if I had had a barium or contrast x-ray recently.

Wearing a hospital gown I had to lie on a padded table and a machine moved backwards and forwards over my body. It was painless and only took about twenty minutes. I was guessing this test was done for my mast cell disease because Megan said a bone density test is sometimes referred to as a bone mass measurement test, measuring bone density and estimating how much bone there was in my hips, spine and other bones throughout the body.

To my surprise, when they had finished that test Megan told me I was booked in for a CT scan but we had an hour and a half to wait for the next appointment so we walked back up to the hotel.

I met Megan in the x-ray department for my CT scan, while Matthew stayed in the hotel as he didn't really see any point in coming with me. I was taken into an x-ray room that had a scanner set up. It was a large machine, shaped like a doughnut at the top of a bed. I had to lie flat on my back and, once I was in the correct position, the radiographer injected a dye solution into the cannula on the back of my hand, to help show up body tissues more clearly on the scan. He told me I would get a hot flushed feeling as the injection entered the blood stream and it would only last for couple of minutes. What he didn't tell me was that I would have the sensation of peeing myself, which made me panic. I felt so embarrassed telling them but they just smiled and said that it was a normal side effect.

The radiographer and Megan left the room to stand behind a glass screen and I was left alone staring up at this machine. The radiographer spoke to me through an intercom and told me he could see me on a TV monitor and he would be controlling the position of the bed from the little room he was in then told me they were about to start the scanner. I was told not to move as the scanner started to spin inside the machine above my head and then began to move slowly over my body.

The scanner took a series of pictures from different angles and gave a picture of slices through the parts of my body being scanned so they could then get a detailed picture of the body.

Together, those cross sections could give a very accurate picture of the size and location of the tumour. The scan took about thirty minutes and would have been painless if I hadn't had my previous back injury, I felt so uncomfortable and after lying on my back for the bone density scan and now the CT scan my back was aching and I couldn't wait for the scan to be over. I was glad when Megan told me I could get dressed and gave me my appointments for the following day.

A needle biopsy was booked for eleven o'clock and a bone marrow biopsy for two o'clock and Megan advised me to bring Matthew with me for support.

When I walked into the reception area to leave the clinic, Matthew was waiting for me. He had been worried as it was now four thirty and he hadn't expected the bone density scan to take so long. Poor Matthew he didn't know about the CT scan.

Chapter Twenty Six

When we got back to the hotel, we went straight to our room as I was in need of some pain killers for my back. I entered the room first and was stopped in my tracks when I saw a snake lying on the bed; it was big and coiled up with its big triangular shaped head raised and I could feel it's eye staring at us. It was a dark colour with diamond shaped patterns across its body and its tail had black and white bands that started to rattle. Matthew grabbed my arm and pulled me out of the room, banging the door shut behind us.

We ran to reception and reported it to the man on the desk, who told us not to go back into the room and to wait in reception while they called the wildlife control. Matthew was excited about the snake and wanted to watch the wildlife control capture and remove it from our room. I didn't find anything exciting about it. Snakes terrified me and I didn't want to see any more.

We went to the hotel bar while we waited for the wildlife control to arrive, the bar tender told us snakes would often wander into the hotel rooms. He said guests would leave the patio doors open and they would just crawl in. I had seen the notice in the room about snakes and about not leaving the doors open but I didn't think anything of it.

The wildlife control arrived within half an hour and Matthew asked them if it was ok for him to go with them. They entered the room and Matthew said the snake was no longer on the bed and he was told to stay by the door. Two men started searching the room and found the snake under the bed.

They told Matthew it was a Western Diamondback rattlesnake and was about four feet long. They told him they were going to trap the snake and, due to the type and size of snake they had to be careful, as it was very dangerous.

They laid a big crate on the ground and placed two dead mice in the centre of it then placed it near to the bed and waited for the snake to crawl out from under the bed and over the side of the crate to get the mice. Once the rest of its body was completely in the crate then they secured the lid on top of it.

They carried the large crate out of the room and put it in the back of their van telling Matthew the snake would be released back into the desert a good distance away from the hotel.

The hotel staff completely cleaned our room again and put fresh bedding on the bed but it didn't stop me making Matthew check around the room and under the bed every time we went in.

Chapter Twenty Seven

Wednesday morning and we walked the short distance in the sun to the clinic for my appointments. I had experienced a needle biopsy before at the Kent Cancer Centre but had no idea what to expect with the bone marrow biopsy. I was told not eat or drink anything for two hours before my appointment and my mouth was dry. My name was called bang on eleven o'clock and Megan showed me into the treatment room. Matthew came with me, as I needed him by my side.

Nathan explained the needle biopsy to me, saying he would inject the skin around the area to numb it then insert a needle through the skin to collect cell samples from the tumour. Pretty much the same as Dr Nayar did but this time Nathan was going to give me something to sedate me, not put me to sleep, just relax me.

It was all over in ten minutes and I didn't feel a thing. I was allowed to go back to the hotel, have something light to eat and a drink then return to the clinic at two o'clock for the bone marrow biopsy and this time I was really nervous.

Megan handed me yet another set of forms to fill in and checked my blood pressure and heart rate. Nathan told me the bone marrow biopsy would take slightly longer than the morning's procedure and, as it could be a little distressing and I was already feeling nervous, he injected me with some sedation through the cannula and left Matthew and me alone while it took effect.

I was panicking thinking the sedation hadn't worked but I soon started to relax, feeling as if I had drank a few too many gin and tonics.

I was told to lie on my side with my back facing Nathan. He draped a white sheet over my back and cleaned the area around my hipbone, before injecting the area to numb.

First he wanted to do a bone marrow aspiration, taking a sample of the liquid portion of the bone marrow so he made a small incision to make it easier to insert the needle. When the needle was in place, he attached a syringe and pulled the plunger back to draw the sample into the syringe? He did this several times so he had a few samples.

I thought the sedation had worn off because I could feel it stinging but Nathan said the inside of the bone cannot be numbed so it is normal to feel some discomfort.

The second procedure was the bone marrow biopsy and he used another large needle but this time the needle went back and forth to get deeper into the bone containing the core of marrow, then he withdrew the needle with the sample, repeating the process on the opposite side of my back. This procedure was so painful it had me in tears and I couldn't wait for it to stop.

I had to spend a while in the recovery room where I wasn't allowed to leave until the sedation had worn off so it was late in the evening before we returned to the hotel.

Chapter Twenty Eight

It was Thursday and I didn't have any appointments, Nathan wanted to get all the test results then he would see me on Friday afternoon.

I was missing Melissa and Jessica so I phoned home to check they were all ok. I spoke to Jessica and she was so pleased to hear from me and informed me everything was ok at home. I could hardly get a word in as she was telling me some tale about one of her friends. I missed her and I hated being away from home. I told her it looked like we would be back on the Saturday and gave her a list of things to do before we arrived back. I checked everything was ok with Melissa and Graeme then hung up.

Matthew decided we should make the most of our free day and wanted to drive to see the Grand Canyon.

It was only 230 miles from Phoenix and I had always wanted to see it but never ever thought I would get the opportunity. It was a beautiful day and it felt good being in the car out of the heat.

We left the hotel, driving through the busy morning traffic, and headed north on Hwy 17. It was a beautiful drive, starting off very flat until we got to New River where we began a very steep climb up through Black Canyon. We pulled over into Sunset Point scenic rest area, on the western edge of what they call a mesa "Tabletop Mountain."

We stood on the edge of a vertical drop and took in the fantastic view of a deep canyon below with huge mountains behind. It was a really pretty place and we planned on calling here on the way back if it was around sun set as we could imagine what a beautiful sight it must be.

The highway carried on quite flat until we start to descend into Verde Valley where it heads steeply downhill through a series of bends leading us into Camp Verde. Here we stopped for a bite to eat and a quick visit to the rest room.

Back on the road we began another steep drive up to the top of the Mogollon Rim which marks the southern edge of the Colorado Plateau that extends 200 miles across central Arizona with a 7000 feet elevation where we passed ponderosa pines and elk on the road side.

Arriving in Flagstaff, we filled up with gas as we weren't quite sure where our next gas station would be then we took the Interstate 40 west of Flagstaff until we got to Williams, where we followed the signs for the Grand Canyon Visitors Centre.

We bought a day pass to visit the South Rim of the Grand Canyon National Park and it was worth every penny.

I will never forget my first sight of the Grand Canyon, the scale and extent of it and with the gorge being so vast it had me feeling quite emotional.

There were lots of people there and most of them seemed to be heading down the hiking trails that went along the canyon so we did the same and set off on a well-marked path along the South Rim trail.

It was a gorgeous walk about 8 miles long and we stopped at various viewpoints but 8 miles was too far for me to walk with my back not fully recovered so we cut it short and headed back after a few miles, which was such a shame as we had never walked anywhere so spectacular. We planned to return another time and do a few days hiking.

Walking back to the centre, Matthew surprised me when he suggested we book a helicopter tour so we would get a perfect view of the canyon. Being in a helicopter was a first for me.

We were strapped into the front seat and had to put headphones on so we could hear the pilot talking to us and, when we set off music was playing.

It was a little bit windy and a little bumpy as we flew over the treetops to the canyon. It took my breath away when the music changed from soft music to more dramatic and we flew straight over the rim into the canyon. I was overwhelmed by the powerful landscape, with the Colorado River running along the bottom of the gorge, the layers of rocks towering above.

As we flew through the canyon the pilot told us the canyon was around 5-6 million years old and was 277 miles long and up to 18 miles wide and had a depth of over a mile. 10,000 years ago Native Americans were the first to build settlements within the canyon and in its caves and many other groups followed years later. Over 40 identified rock layers formed the Grand Canyon's walls, making it the colourful sight we see today.

The pilot flew us down along the river bed and back up close to the canyon walls,
It was one of the most magical moments I have ever experienced in my life and a truly amazing sight.

Matthew and I had a fantastic day and finished off with a lovely dinner in the Arizona Room Restaurant before we headed back on our long drive to Phoenix. It was dark when we left and I almost forgot the reason why we had come to Arizona.

Chapter Twenty Nine

Friday morning and today I was to get the results from all my tests and I was hoping Dr Nayar had been right when he said I didn't have cancer.

I couldn't eat breakfast or lunch so by two thirty I was starting to feel a bit shaky and sick. Entering Nathan's office, we found Megan standing next to him and as we walked in he asked how I was feeling and if we had done anything special the previous day. We told him about our nice day out and chatted a little about it.

Nathan then went on to tell us he didn't have all the test results back and gave us no information about the ones that were back.

He said he had booked me into the Weston Hospital in the centre of Phoenix for ten thirty on Saturday morning, where he had arranged for a thoracic surgeon to perform a Mediastinotomy and a Mediastinoscopy with a biopsy, both minor surgical procedures used to gather more samples from the tumour.

I explained I had already had a biopsy done just after my accident in the Willow Royal Hospital and I pulled my t-shirt down at the neck to show him the two-inch scar I had on my chest. He said he would be more satisfied with the diagnosis if their thoracic surgeon performed this procedure and, if it was a cancer tumour, it would give him an idea of how far the cancer had advanced.

We were shocked and told him we had planned to go home the next morning thinking all my tests had been complete, and that we had never expected that I would need surgery. Nathan said he could not give me an accurate second opinion without doing this procedure, and, as we turned to walked out of his office, he handed Matthew an envelope and told him we needed to go to the finance office before we left the clinic.

Not sure what the urgency was, we walked down the stairs to the finance office where a very smart looking lady behind the desk took the envelope from Matthew and guided us into a little office, where we sat down and waited for her to return.

When she came back into the room she was carrying a file and started pulling paperwork from it. She confirmed I was booked for surgery at the Weston Hospital the following morning and handed me some papers to sign and told us we needed to pay for the surgery now otherwise it would not go ahead.

We had not expected this. We were confused, as Matthew was expecting everything to be paid through our private health insurance when we got back to Corby but she repeated that the payment of $13,950 had to be paid that afternoon for my surgery to go ahead.

I was shocked and upset. I had never talked to Matthew about how we were going to pay for the treatment at the clinic and I just assumed Matthew had it all in hand.

I had no idea how we could afford it; we had just used the money out of our savings account to buy the land we were going to build our new house on, so I knew there was no extra cash in our bank accounts and the credit card had taken a bit of a hit while we were staying in Phoenix.

The lady insisted once again on the payment and I started to cry. Matthew excused us for a few minutes from her office and walked me out along the corridor and I told him I was worried about the clinic bill, let alone the cost of the surgery. Matthew tried to calm me down and told me not to worry, that he would make some phone calls and make sure the surgery was paid for.

I walked up the hill to the hotel and threw myself on the bed, crying, and a thought came into mind: I had forgotten to ask Matthew if our private health insurance back in Canada covered us for any costs.

It was over two hours before Matthew returned to the hotel and I had been pacing the room waiting for him. I needed to know what was happening.

Matthew was all cool and relaxed when he came into the room and told me it was all sorted and my surgery was still going ahead the next day. I wanted to know if he had been in touch with our private health insurance company and if they were going to be paying for all my treatment. He said I was not to think about any of it and that it was sorted. He sniggered, saying it was just like another day in the office for him and laughed it off. I was livid. It was no joking matter. I was always the one that worried about money and this was not another business challenge; this was a bill we had to find the money to pay and, as far as I was aware, we didn't have the money to pay it. Not only did I have a cancer diagnosis to deal with I also had the financial worries.

Chapter Thirty

Saturday ten thirty and I arrived at the Weston Hospital where, after booking in at a reception desk, Matthew was told to leave and was handed a card with a phone number to call later so he could enquire how I was.

I was then led to a large waiting room, packed with people from all different cultures. There were no free seats so a teenage boy stood up and offered me his seat. He was very friendly and talked non-stop. I think he was nervous and I felt sorry for him.

I sat there for over an hour before my name was called and the nurse was not as nice as Megan. She gave me a gown to change into and a bag to put my clothes in, which she took away to lock them in a locker. She was a bit bossy and told me off for not having brought any slippers.

I then had to sit in another waiting room full of women, where I waited another hour until I was led to what looked like a holding area full of beds surrounded by curtains, where patients were waiting to be wheeled into theatre.

I was assigned to a bed and the anaesthetist came to explain his role in my surgery; he would be giving me a general anaesthetic that would be injected into my vein via the cannula I still had attached to my hand and he would be staying with me throughout the surgery to make sure I stayed asleep. He had forms I had to sign and he checked the cannula was still in place then left, saying he would see me in theatre.

Then the thoracic surgeon came and introduced himself and told me he would first be doing a Mediastinotomy where he would make an incision on my chest where my previous scar was to give him entry to the part of the mediastinum that was not accessible with a Mediastinoscopy and he would take pieces of the mass for examination.

The Mediastinoscopy would be done next, where a small incision would be made into my throat where he could insert a mediastinoscope, a tube with a camera fitted to the end, linked up to a monitor so he could see pictures of my chest, where he could see to take the rest of the samples he needed.

He told me I was in safe hands and I signed some forms and was once again left on my own. I was so nervous; my heart was pounding so fast, I was feeling sick and felt short of breath. I was frightened. I wished Matthew was with me to reassure me everything would be ok. A nurse came to my bedside and I started to cry. I felt so embarrassed acting like a child. The nurse gave me a couple of tablets to help calm me down and about twenty minutes later two nurses came and wheeled me into theatre.

Lying on the theatre bed I could see lights shining down on me with lots of faces covered in masks. The anaesthetist sat by my head and started to insert the injection into the cannula then put a black mask over my nose and mouth and I felt myself drift off to sleep.

Chapter Thirty One

I could hear someone talking to me, saying, "Lisa, wake up" she kept repeating it and I wasn't sure if I was dreaming or if I was awake. I tried hard to open my eyes but I still couldn't, I could still hear the voice, "Lisa, Lisa wake up" then I could feel myself coming round and everything started to come into focus.

I felt groggy and really sick. I tried to speak but I had an oxygen mask over my nose and mouth I pulled it away and the words came out in a whisper, I needed a drink. My throat was so sore and my mouth dry. The nurse put a straw to my mouth and I took a sip of water, feeling the pain as it went down my throat and I fell back into a deep sleep.

It was late afternoon when I finally woke up and felt fully awake. I was in the recovery room and attached to a heart and circulation monitor. I had a chest drain in and I was catheterized and I was also was wearing compression socks. A nurse standing beside me checked my vital signs and told me I would be transferred onto the ward now I was awake.

I must have dozed off again because when I woke I was in a room on my own, very similar to the room at the Willow Royal in Corby but this time there were no cards or flowers.

My chest was sore so the nurse gave me some morphine which made me sick so she gave me some anti-sickness tablets. I was in a right state and I felt awful. Eventually everything calmed down and I slept through the night.

Mathew arrived the following morning and I was sitting up in bed feeling much better. I had even enjoyed my breakfast of cereal and toast. Nathan entered my room shortly after Matthew and asked how I was feeling and told me the operation had gone well and he now had all the test results and the biopsy result. It wasn't good news. He confirmed I did have cancer.

He said I was to stay in hospital until the following day and then see him in his office at three o'clock, when he would explain everything. I was devastated, I really hoped Dr Nayar had been right when he told me I didn't have cancer. How could this be happening to me again? Nathan left me to digest the news but, before he left, he said "Its 16th April today so happy birthday, Lisa."

Chapter Thirty Two

My 42nd birthday and I was lying in a hospital bed miles away from my family and having been told for the second time in four months that I had cancer.

I was furious with Dr Nayar for telling me I didn't have cancer and now having to go through all this again. Matthew was also upset but I was in no mood for him. I needed to be on my own so I told him to leave. He didn't want to go but I insisted, shouting at him as he walked out the door. Matthew had asked the nurse to check on me but I didn't want to talk to her either. I cried until I couldn't cry any more.

My life was once again turning upside down and I wondered why this was happening to me.

In the past four months I had had a horrible skiing accident, suffered with a broken back, been told I had cancer, been told I didn't have cancer and now, after a week of tests being told I do have cancer and, on top of that I was worried about paying the Weston Clinic bill. How much more could I take?

That was the worse birthday I have ever had. I was 42, still young and still fit. There were so many things I still wanted to do in life and I thought back to how happy I had been when I joined the running club back in Cumbria.

I had been watching the London marathon on TV and I was so inspired by all the runners and as soon as it finished I put my shorts and trainers on and ran two miles down the road and back.

I was 34 and was enjoying running four miles twice a week. On one of my runs, I ran round a corner into four men who were running just in front of me. One of them was my GP so I ran alongside them, chatting.

They told me they ran for the local running club and that I should join, so at the next training session I turned up for my first club night and ran with about seven women who were all so nice, I really enjoyed it but they told me I ran at a faster pace than them and suggested I ran with the men.

The next club night I joined twenty men to run seven miles on wet country roads in the rain. Being the only girl, I was determined not to hold them back and I pushed myself hard to keep up with the middle group. They were a great bunch of guys, always encouraging me and giving me the motivation to keep turning up for club nights.

After buying some new running shoes, I entered my first race, the windmill half marathon in Lytham St Ann's, which turned out to be such an enjoyable run.

I went on to run many 10k races and some fell races. I was so competitive I would pick out certain guys from the club and push myself to try and beat them in a race.

I was hooked and obsessed with running. I stopped buying my usual girl magazine and started buying running magazines. I felt for the first time since I was married and had children that I was doing something for me and it felt good.

The following year, on April 25th 1993, after a few months of training with our club running coach and running ten miles four times a week then meeting some of the guys on a Saturday morning to run eighteen to twenty miles, I ran the Paris marathon.

A coach full of us left the running club for the long drive to Paris and everyone was in high spirits. We had all trained hard and were ready for the race.

We lined up in front of the Arc de Triomphe, all grouped together and, when the horn blew to start the race, we set off running down towards the Place de la Concorde and from there we ran round the city, going through various parks.

It was a hard, enjoyable race and I paced myself just as our club trainer had told me to. I never hit the wall that everyone talks about when they run a marathon and, as I came round the corner with the Eiffel Tower in front of me showing me the end of the race was in sight, I saw one of the guys from our running club just in front of me, I ran up to him and tapped him on the shoulder as I ran past him and we raced to the finish together, with him just beating me.

I ran the race in 3hrs 50 minutes and I was so proud of myself. It was one of the most challenging things I had ever done. I ran it in aid of cancer research and spent weeks getting people to sponsor me. There was even an article in the local evening news about it. Little did I know that year's later cancer would play a bigger part in my life?

Chapter Thirty Three

I felt so sad and alone lying there in that bed and the next morning Matthew didn't find me feeling any better. I was in a foul mood and was feeling sore and tired from my surgery. Matthew didn't say much to me; I think he was frightened I'd bite his head off.

When I was getting dressed and packing my bag to leave, the nurse handed me the box of tissues that was next to my bed and the shampoo and shower gel out of the bathroom. I told her I didn't want them and she said I should take them because they had been added to my hospital bill. Then she handed me a copy of the invoice and everything for my surgery and stay in hospital was itemized and she was right they were there on the list.

Nathan certainly was a good doctor. He was such a lovely man, very professional and had a nice caring manner and he made sure I was calm before he started to tell me about the results.

First he told me I had done the right thing listening to and acting on my gut feelings and going to the Weston Clinic for a second opinion. The results from all the tests did show I had systemic mastocytosis, which is a very rare mast cell disease. The mast cells are innate cells whose job is to defend the body against bacteria, viruses and parasites and to play a part in our allergic response. Mast cells can release too much histamine into the body, which can give us the allergic reactions and anaphylactic shocks. He confirmed that the only treatment for this was antihistamines and recommended I have regular blood and urine checks. Secondly, the test results showed I had nodular sclerosing Hodgkin's disease and it was stage 1A. He said nodular sclerosing was the most common type of Hodgkin's lymphoma and stage 1A meant that the cancer was limited to the tumour on my mediastinum and that I didn't have many significant symptoms.

He showed me the tumour on the CT results and it looked the size of a small lemon. He told me they couldn't remove the tumour because of its position and the best treatment would be to destroy as many cancer cells as possible.

He gave me two choices of different ways of treatment; first I could go down the road of chemotherapy or, due to me being a perfect candidate, I could go on experimental drugs.

I know cancer needs to be researched, as well as treatment, but there was no way I was going to risk my recovery so I told him I would prefer going down the chemotherapy route.

He recommended I have chemotherapy followed by radiation therapy. The chemotherapy was used to kill lymphoma cells and would consist of four drugs, Adriamycin, Bleomycin, Vinblastine and Dacarbazine (ABVD) and that would be given to me in cycles. After completing the course of chemotherapy, I would start radiation therapy to help kill off the Hodgkin's disease cells.

He told me it would be a tough few months for me but, with all this treatment, he hoped it would put my cancer into remission. If I hadn't got the second opinion and therefore the treatment, I would only have survived another two years.

He said I would have to return to the Kent Cancer Centre to have my treatment and he would write to them stipulating what treatment I should have. The last thing I wanted was to go back to the Kent Cancer Centre; I was so annoyed at them for misdiagnosing me but Nathan told me he would make sure he put in his report that I should be seen by a different oncologist.

He told me to go home and I would hear from the Kent Cancer Centre when I was to start my treated. I thanked Nathan for all his help and he wished me luck and hoped everything went well for me.

We had been in Phoenix for ten days and our flight out was at seven o'clock that night. I wasn't in the mood for talking and I didn't think Matthew knew what to say to me so we didn't speak all the way home. I just looked out of the aeroplane window into the darkness and all I could think about was that, once again, I had to tell my daughters I have cancer.

This was so unfair. I felt like I had a curse over me. The tears rolled down my cheeks and, in silence, I asked my dad to watch over me and wished he was still alive to help me get through this.

Chapter Thirty Four

It was the middle of the night when we arrived home and everyone was in bed, Matthew lifted the bags upstairs and went to bed. There was no way I was going to sleep so I put another log on the fire and poured myself a large glass of red wine and sat on the rug in the darkness watching the wood catch fire.

Jessica woke me the next morning and I was curled up on the sofa with the throw over me. The house came alive when Melissa and Graeme came into the kitchen and Matthew wandered down from upstairs.

I started making coffee and popping slices of bread in the toaster. The girls gave me belated birthday cards and presents and said how sad they had been that I hadn't got back home for my birthday. They had baked a cake and showed me the few slices that were left, and I thought, "That's the second birthday spoiled so far this year."

Jessica had turned eighteen on the 27th February and normally I would have thrown a party for her and her friends but I was still recovering from my fractured back and was not well enough to do anything special and poor Jessica missed out.

When we were all sat round the table having breakfast I told them about the tests and surgery that happened in Phoenix and broke the news about the cancer being re-diagnosed.

They were all upset but told me they had expected that to be the outcome and were already prepared for the news. Matthew and Graeme went to work and Jessica went to school, Melissa had home study so there were only the two of us at home.

I was trying not to be down and kept myself busy tidying the house. The girls weren't the best at housework and, after being on their own for ten days, there was a lot to do.

Around midday the doorbell rang and our next-door neighbour, who was not a very nice woman, was standing on the porch. She didn't like us and, since we moved in, she had done nothing but complain about various things. She started shouting at me, telling me I was an irresponsible mother for leaving my family on their own while I was away enjoying a holiday and that my kids had been causing trouble. She said my girls had friends to stay and had been playing their music really loud and had been drinking and shouting and swearing on the back deck. I apologised for them disturbing her but reminded her they were all over the age of eighteen and old enough to drink and to be left on their own and that they would never do anything deliberately to upset her.

She got even angrier and told me Jessica had tried to burn her house down and she had to call the fire service. I was mortified. There was no way Jessica would do something like that and I told her so.

Melissa came out of the house after hearing all the commotion and I asked her what had been going on and if Jessica had tried to burn our neighbour's house down. Melissa said it wasn't true. Jessica didn't do anything on purpose. She had been smoking on the front porch with her girlfriends and they threw the cigarette butts onto the grass next to our neighbour's house and, with it being dry it started to smoulder and the fire truck came and threw a bucket of water on it to dampen it down.

I once again apologised to our neighbour and told her I would have words with Jessica. I was so angry with Jessica, not only for what she had done to the neighbour but because I didn't even know she smoked. How could she smoke when I was going through cancer?

When school was due to finish I drove to pick her up and she was surprised to see me sitting in my car waiting for her. She was even more surprised when she saw how angry I was. I told her about the neighbour's complaint and how disappointed I was with her and that she had to go round and apologise. Then I gave her a lecture about smoking. When Matthew came home and heard about it he went mad with Jessica and she stayed in her room all night.

Matthew was even more angry with our neighbour for coming round the minute we were home he said she should have gone to him about it and not upset me, that I had enough to deal with. I explained she didn't know I had cancer and she was within her rights to complain and he said he had been speaking to her the day before we left for Phoenix and told her why we were going. She knew we were not on a holiday and he slammed the door as he walked out the house to speak to her.

All this upset was something I did not need and it looked like having cancer wouldn't change every day issues.

Chapter Thirty Five

A couple of weeks had gone by after returning from Phoenix and I couldn't settle, I wasn't sleeping very well and I was having very strange dreams.

I had an appointment for Tuesday May 9th to see a Dr Alex Wheeldon, a haematologist oncologist at the Kent Cancer Centre and we had a date for Friday 2nd June to complete on the house. Jessica had the last of her school exams the week of 15th May then she would be done with school and Melissa had her final course exams 23rd, 24th and 25th of May.

Matthew was constantly showing me updated house plans that he was going through with the builder and my poor mum was so worried about me she was never off the phone, still wanting to book a flight to come over.

I was finding it all too much but didn't say anything to anyone and I told my mum she had to wait until things had settled down.

Dr Wheeldon was a short stocky man with dark hair. He was very professional and not as friendly as Nathan had been at the Weston.

He explained he had the report from the Weston Clinic with the results from all the tests they had done and the treatment programme Dr Warwick had set out for me. He said I was to start chemotherapy the following Monday, 8th May, which would consist of the four chemotherapy drugs ABVD - Adriamycin, Bleomycin, Vinblastine and Dacarbazine - done in three cycles, followed by radiotherapy. He handed me a sheet with a list of my treatment plan.

Chemotherapy ABVD

1st cycle start 8th May for four weeks Monday-Friday.

2nd cycle start 12th June for four weeks Monday-Friday.

3rd cycle start 17th July for four weeks Monday-Friday.

With two weeks rest in between.

16th August Moulds and shields to be made for radiotherapy.

Radiotherapy starts

1st cycle 28th August every day for four weeks

One month rest

2nd cycle 23rd October, every day for four weeks

He said it was a lot of treatment for me to undergo and he would have suggested having either chemotherapy or radiotherapy and not both but, as Dr Warwick had set the treatment plan, they would do as he instructed. He told me that, on the day I would start my chemotherapy treatment, there would be a bed available for me on the chemotherapy day unit.

He prescribed me a batch of antihistamines to help control my Mast Cell Disease and told me I would be called back for regular check-ups.

I left his office looking again at the treatment plan, hoping that would save my life and, for the first time, I realised I had a massive battle on my hands. Year 2000 was turning out to be a hard year.

Chapter Thirty Six

In the days leading up to my treatment I was very down. It had been two and a half years since we left Cumbria to live in Canada and I had never felt so alone.

I didn't have any friends in Canada, my life revolved around Matthew and the girls. I missed my old life, I missed my family and friends. I missed driving to Carlisle every month to see my mum where we'd go shopping, stopping for coffee in Marks and Spencer's. I was very close to my younger brother, Daniel, and I missed our fun times together. I missed the running club and everyone in it, my afternoons meeting my girlfriends for lunch, gossiping, putting the world to rights and supporting each other when we had a problem.

I didn't have my friend Linda turning up on the doorstep in need of a coffee and chat. I missed my dear friend Paul whom I would run with on non-club nights. He wasn't as good a runner as me but we enjoyed each other's company as I'd make him race me down the canal on a frosty night. I missed going to work every day at the doctor's surgery where, every morning someone had a story to tell and where Val and I bonded like sisters. I missed going to the local pub straight from work on a Friday night to meet friends where we all sat in the same seats and laughed at the same stupid jokes. I missed doing my shopping in the market square on a Saturday afternoon and bumping into people I knew. I missed it all. Back then I had been an individual person, where in Canada I was just a wife and a mum.

If I had to choose again I would have never given that life up. Matthew made emigrating sound so exciting but, in reality, it was a lonely life for me and now, having to fight cancer, I felt I needed everyone back in my life.

When Matthew was offered the job in Canada he didn't take any persuading to accept it.

He received a phone call from the Canadian company that was headhunting him and when he finished the call, he told me they had offered him a job and they were going to give him a day or two to think about it.

When they called him back they offered to pay to fly us all out to Canada for a week so he could see where he would be working and let us get a feel for what life was like but, other than wanting to discuss salary and a relocation package, he just accepted the job and handing in his notice.

He was never allowed back in his office and what personal items were there were boxed up by the secretary and dropped off at our house.

Three weeks later on the 1st October, Matthew left us for Canada, leaving me to deal with the upset of two daughters not wanting to move away. My ex-husband, the girls' dad was not happy that he wasn't going to see much of them and would come round to my house in tears. I had to sell the house, sell the car, sell all electrical goods and pack the house up for shipping everything overseas.

I had to find a rented, furnished house for the girls and me to live in until they had finished school the following July. I really felt Matthew had it easy and sometimes think if I had told him in the nine months we were apart that I didn't want to move to Canada he would have stayed there without me.

I needed to shake off this mood so I decided to go right through the house and clean it so everything was done before my treatment started. I chose a day when everyone was out so I could have no distractions. I loved to listen to music when I was alone in the house and especially when I was doing housework so I pulled out one of my favourite cd's and turned the music system up loud and sang along to every song as I busied myself around the house.

When a song about angels came on it stopped me in my tracks. I had heard that song so many times before but I had never heard it like I did that day.

I could have sworn it was my dad singing every word of the lyrics to me, and as I stood looking out of the window listening to every word. I cried like I had never cried before.

The one person I missed the most was my dad and he was the one man I wanted right at that moment. I believed he was trying to send me a message and I played that song over and over again whenever I was on my own and it would always make me feel he was close to me.

Chapter Thirty Seven

Monday 8th May was the start of a journey I never thought I would have to take. I never thought I would get cancer and become a cancer victim.

We take life so much for granted, we sail on through, never expecting anything to harm us and it's frightening how fast your life can change. Now I wanted my life to change again so I could be a cancer survivor and if that meant I had to fight with everything I had then that's exactly what I would do.

Melissa drove me to the Kent Cancer Centre for my chemotherapy treatment, I had no idea what it entailed other than what I had seen on some TV hospital drama. I'm not squeamish and my pain threshold went up a few notches from recovering from my broken back but I was scared.

Nathan told me in Phoenix that, if I had a choice which cancer to have this was the one to pick. He said it's known as "the good cancer," that Hodgkin's is very treatable and the one that gives the best chance of survival, with many cases being cured. That was all well and good but how could it be good when chasing a cure meant several months of chemotherapy followed by two months of radiation therapy with no guarantee it would work, not to mention the emotional impact of it all. If I did survive, every time I got an ache or sweat in bed at night would I go into a panic thinking the cancer had come back? So no I didn't think this was a good cancer, I don't think any cancer is good. I thought cancer would change me for the rest of my life.

The first person I met at the clinic was Suzie, the phlebotomist, a bright and bubbly lady in her forties, who explained that on my treatment days I would see her first, when she would take blood samples to check I was ok to have chemotherapy. Then I had to wait in the waiting room while the bloods were checked. When they were back from the lab, I was called back into the treatment room where a nurse called Jolene took my weight and blood pressure before Dr Wheeldon came in to tell me my bloods were all ok and I could start my chemo.

Jolene then took me to the Chemotherapy Day Unit, a big bright room with a row of chairs on one side and on the other a row of beds, I was shown to a bed in the middle of the row.

I didn't have to get undressed and was told I could sit on top of the bed. Melissa sat on the comfy chair next to the bed. She had brought her course work so she could revise for her exams while she waited for my treatment to finish.

A pretty nurse called Cathy, who I think was also in her thirties, told me she would be looking after me each time I attended the unit. She was very nice and very professional. First, she injected an anti-sickness drug through the cannula into the vein, then the first of the chemotherapy drugs, a red fluid called Doxorubicin (Adriamycin) which was pumped through my vein as a slow drip. Cathy called this drug " the red devil" as it's the one that hits the cancer cells the hardest and is used to treat other cancers by stopping the fast growing cancer cells from making new cells and it also stops the damaged cancer cells from continuing to grow.

As it was going in, I could feel pain and burning along the vein so Cathy slowed the drip down even further which made it more comfortable. This drug turns your pee red and I would have been in a panic if Cathy hadn't warned me about it, telling me it was normal and wouldn't cause me any problems. As the drug was going through my system the only side effect I got from it, apart from the red pee, was a horrible taste in my mouth. Everything I ate or drank tasted foul. Cathy sent Melissa out to buy me some sour-flavoured candy, saying they would help.

When that drug was finished Cathy attached a bag of saline and turned the speed of the pump up so it would flush the line for my next chemo drug, called Bleomycin, or "Bleo" as

Cathy called it. This was a clear fluid and is a type of antibiotic that is poisonous to cells. It binds the cancer cells so that they can't divide or grow, this drug was also administrated pumped through a slow drip.

The morning seemed to fly in and, before I knew it, I was being offered sandwiches and soup for my lunch but I really didn't feel like eating I was starting to feel a bit nauseous so I gave Melissa my lunch.

I was so glad of Melissa's company. She didn't get much revision done as she was too interested in what was going on in the unit and talking to other patients and making sure I was ok.

The chairs opposite were all full with men and women connected to drips, most of them a bit older than me. Some of the ladies had colourful bandanas on their heads. Two had nothing and were showing their shiny bald heads and one poor elderly lady had a curly wig which was so obvious, I felt sorry for her. Surely someone could have helped her choose one that was more natural.

The beds on my side were also full and in the bed next to me was a young man of nineteen, called Jamie. He enjoyed talking to us, especially Melissa, showing an interest in her course work and her plans to be a paramedic.

He told us he was at The University of Lethbridge studying to be a lawyer but his treatment had made him miss a few weeks. He had quite advanced Hodgkin's lymphoma stage 4 and was having similar treatment to me.

He was by himself and said his dad had dropped him off on his way to work and would collect him later and that he didn't mind because his dad fussed over him too much. I liked Jamie he was so upbeat and positive, he would joke about with the nurses and make Melissa and me laugh.

My third drug was Vinblastine which is sometimes called microtubule inhibitors, describing the way it works by damaging cancer cells by stopping them from separating into two new cells and blocking the growth of cancer.

This drug seemed to go through my system more easily than the previous two but, by the end of it, Melissa said I was starting to look very pale and tired.

Cathy flushed with saline again before starting with the fourth chemo drug. This one was called Dacarbazine and Cathy gave me another anti-sickness injection before she started pumping it through my veins. She told me this was the worst of the four drugs and that was why she gave it to me last.

Dacarbazine belongs to a group of medicines called alkylating agents and it interferes with the growth of cancer cells, which are eventually destroyed. It can lower blood cells that help your body fight infections and help your blood to clot so you can get an infection or bleed more easily. I had therefore to avoid being near people who were sick or had infection. Something else I didn't know was that this drug was likely to make my hair fall out.

I was now feeling the effects of all the four drugs and lay under the covers on the bed. Melissa handed me a bowl just in time for me to be sick and I felt dreadful. I wasn't in the mood for chatting anymore and I noticed Jamie had also gone quiet. Melissa kept asking both of us if we were ok.

A few hours later and after another saline flush I was ready to go home. We had been in there all day and I can honestly say I did not enjoy a single minute of that treatment and can sympathise and empathise with anyone who has to go through it.

Chapter Thirty Eight

Back at home Matthew, had made supper but I didn't want any; I felt exhausted and went straight to bed. Cathy had given me some anti-sickness tablets to bring home to help me cope with the nausea and vomiting and, after the vomiting stopped, I slept most of the night, not even hearing Matthew coming to bed.

When I got out of bed the next morning to go to the bathroom I could hardly put one foot in front of the other, I felt that running my marathon in Paris was easier than walking to the bathroom. I constantly felt nauseous, couldn't eat, and wasn't even hungry.

Matthew went to work, dropping Jessica off at school. I was again left with Melissa taking care of me, trying her best to make me eat and drink something. My body was flushed red all over and my face was puffy and hot.

My temperature started to rise and I had cold chills so Melissa called the help line, to be told that they were common side effects and should pass and to keep me hydrated.

Wednesday found my body still hot and red and I was exhausted, I mean really exhausted not the kind of exhaustion you feel after a busy week at work or a week with no sleep or even the last twenty steps of climbing up a mountain. It was much more powerful than that but at least my temperature had dropped.

Thursday my fingers and hands kept going numb. Poor Melissa was again concerned and called the help line again and was told this was due to the Vinblastine chemo drug as it can give you nerve damage.

My mind started to play tricks on me and I couldn't concentrate or remember things like people's names and I couldn't finish my sentences. I wasn't interested in anything Matthew or the girls were saying and I wouldn't speak to my mum when Melissa came into the bedroom with the phone in her hand saying my mum was on the phone.

By Saturday I was starting to recover but the tiredness was still there. Matthew had men clearing the trees from our new piece of land and wanted to go and check how they were getting on and insisted I was to go with him.

After an hour of driving we had left the city behind and were now in the country, full of prairie fields and land that had turned green after being buried under snow for five months of the winter.

Growing up as a country girl, I loved the space and quietness that our land had to offer, not forgetting the wildlife that was there. I was never too keen on City living - there are too many people and buildings, the shops are always crowded and everyone seems to rush about as if they are running out of time for whatever it is they need to do.

I was looking forward to setting up a new home for all of us, knowing the girls and Graeme would love it out there. As we turned the corner to enter our land I could hear the chainsaws going, where four men were busy taking trees down to make a big enough clearing for the house to be built on.

The sun was bright in the sky and it was lovely and warm as we all sat on the trunk of a tree that had just been flattened to the ground and the four men were grateful for the hot coffee and sandwiches I had made for them.

It was so nice to be out in the fresh air and walking through the land. We found a path that the deer had made through the trees and, as we walked along it, we could hear animals running through the bushes and we saw a deer run right across the path about ten yards in front of us. The path led us all the way down to the river and we sat on the riverbank watching the water run fast past us. There was a beaver's den to one side of the river and the beaver was swimming alongside it. Fish were leaping out of the water catching insects. Some of them were quite big and would make a big splash, leaving numerous ripples on the water.

We heard a rustle behind us and I jumped thinking it might be a bear sneaking up on us but it wasn't. It was a huge porcupine with a pointed nose and spiky back. He walked past us, and climbed up a tree and sat in the sun on a high branch. We were fascinated having never seen a porcupine before and I didn't know they climbed trees.

Walking back up the hill was hard for me and I soon ran out of energy. Matthew had to almost drag me up by my arms but it had been worth the walk down to the river and I was looking forward to spending more time down there after our house was built.

Sunday I managed to enjoy some breakfast sitting round the table with Matthew, Melissa, Graeme and Jessica but the rest of the day I was wiped out and Jessica and I sat on the sofa watching movies.

Monday was the start of my week's rest before the next chemo session started and this was to be my so called good week so I had planned to catch up on the house work, do the laundry and ironing and cook some yummy meals for the family but I found it hard to drag myself out of bed.

I couldn't believe I was still feeling so tired but, once I was out of bed, I made a big effort to tackle my list of jobs and ended up doing very little and needing to rest up all afternoon. I guess I was wrong thinking my energy would return on my good week and I would be back to normal. That didn't seem to be the case and I needed to rest more than I expected.

Jessica had her school exams that week so she was stressed out. She hated exams. She lacked confidence in herself and would panic the minute she opened the exam sheet. There was nothing I could say to her to make her feel more relaxed about it.

Friday was her last day of exams so I baked her a cake and Matthew cooked on the BBQ and we all sat outside on the deck enjoying the evening sunshine and she looked more herself now, she had her first week of exams behind her. Sunday I got a sinking feeling knowing I was about to start the whole chemotherapy process over again.

Chapter Thirty Nine

Monday morning and it was week two of my chemo and once again I had Melissa for company. Jolene checked my blood pressure and weight and Suzie attached another cannula, using a different vein and took blood samples for testing.

Dr Wheeldon gave me the all clear from my bloods but told me I had to have a white blood count booster to keep me on track with my chemotherapy plan because, if my white blood cell count dropped, my chemo would be delayed. I was given the drug to take home and I had to inject it into myself at home in between my next rounds of chemo.

Cathy led me to the same bed I had had the previous week and hooked me up to a pump again to start my treatment. Jamie called across to us from his bed and we exchanged stories about our past two weeks of chemo symptoms.

The day unit didn't seem to be the same that week. The patients opposite me in the chairs didn't seem to be in a chatty mood and sat with their eyes closed with sad looks on their faces. A man opposite was having a problem with one of the chemo drugs burning his vein and the nurse was trying to make him more comfortable. The nurses all seemed to be busier that week and had less time to talk. Even Jamie didn't stay bubbly for very long.

Knowing what to expect didn't make it any easier. I dreaded the drugs being pumped through my body with all those toxins attacking my cells. I too wasn't as chatty as I had been the week before; even making conversation with Melissa was hard work so she just sat quietly by my bed, doing some last minute revision for her exams.

I was starting to have a reaction to certain smells and it was getting worse. Now the alcohol swabs were turning my stomach, making me cover my nose and breathe through my mouth. By the afternoon, I was vomiting again and lying in the bed feeling weak.

Melissa tucked me into bed when we got home, as the side effects of the treatment were starting to take hold and all I wanted was to be in bed and to close the door on the world.

The next morning I felt like an emotional wreck. I kept bursting out in tears for no reason and had to cut short a conversation with my mum because I was going to cry. The only time I got out of bed was to go to the bathroom. I didn't even have any energy to stand under the shower.

Melissa started her exams today and as much as I tried to put a brave face on for her she could see right through me and left the house worrying. Jessica was at home as there was no school for her that day. She was coming to the end of her exams with only one more to do. I didn't see much of her other than bringing me some lunch and popping up stairs to ask the odd question but I didn't mind. I was having a bad day and I didn't really want any company.

Matthew was not in the best of moods when he got home from work and basically ignored me when he came in to the bedroom to change from his office clothes into his jeans and t-shirt. He didn't even ask how I was feeling and walked out of the bedroom without saying a word.

Something was obviously wrong and I knew I hadn't upset him so I called after him but he didn't answer and I heard his footsteps going down the stairs to the kitchen. It wasn't like Matthew to be like that so I dragged myself out of bed wrapped my dressing gown around me and headed down stairs.

I could hear Matthew shouting at Jessica but about what I had no idea. Jessica passed me on the stairs as she stormed into her bedroom and, when I asked Matthew what she had done wrong, he just shrugged his shoulders and said nothing.

I went into Jessica's bedroom and found her crying and I asked her what was wrong. She said that, as soon as she started to talk to Matthew, he started to shout at her and, when she asked him what was wrong, he said he was fed up coming home to her leaving dishes on the kitchen counter instead of putting them in the dishwasher. From there, it turned into a shouting match between them both, with Matthew saying she was always causing trouble.

Matthew and Jessica had never got along and could wind each other up. I was always the one in the middle, keeping the peace between them, and today it looked like Matthew was the one in the wrong, being grumpy after a bad day at the office and he was taking it out on poor Jessica. Not that he would admit to it.

I was not in the mood for an argument with Matthew but I wanted to get to the bottom of it so I poured him a large glass of wine, even though the smell of the wine was making me feel nauseous and made him tell me what was wrong.

He told me he had found out that our private health insurance was not going to cover the medical bills from the Weston Clinic in Phoenix so he had been in touch with our local health authority and they wouldn't cover it either. They told him they wouldn't pay for out of country medical expenses and that we should have informed them about our plans to go to the United States for a second opinion before we left. They would have arranged for a second opinion with another cancer centre in another city in our own province or maybe another province in Canada. They didn't see the need to go out of the country when there were oncologists who could do the same for me in Canada.

I thought Matthew had already dealt with the clinic payment. I didn't even know how much it was and I nearly fell off my chair when he told me the total cost was forty thousand dollars. Where on earth were we supposed to get that amount of money from? I asked him how it came to be such a big amount. He told me it included the flight tickets over, the hire car, the hotel bill of 10 days stay, meals and the bill for the Weston

Clinic and the Weston Hospital where I had my operation.

Matthew had paid the amount but he had to max out our credit card and take out a bridging loan from the bank to pay the rest. We were now paying daily interest until it was paid off and we had no money to pay it. Matthew said he had been trying to sort it without me knowing anything but he couldn't and thought the only thing for us to do was get a lawyer and sue the Kent Cancer centre for misdiagnosis.

As much as I was upset that Dr Nayar had messed up with diagnosing my cancer, I had no intentions of suing him or the clinic. After all, I was now getting the treatment I needed. I was so shocked and I didn't have any energy left to deal with this. I just wanted to crawl back into bed, pull the duvet over my head and forget this was happening.

I suggested we change the house plans and build something smaller and cheaper. Let's face it, why did we need a 4,000 square foot executive house?

We went over the plans to see where we could cut back. It was to have a spacious open plan ground floor with a large living room, a featured wood burning stove, a beech wood spiral staircase leading to the upper floor, a dining area with window seats and a luxury, top of the range, gourmet kitchen with state of the art appliances.

From the living room there would be access through patio doors to a spa room with a sunken hot tub surrounded by glass walls and patio doors.

All the ground floor was to have maple hardwood floors and big arched windows with special glass to keep the cold out and the heat in.

Upstairs was to have three big bedrooms with an amazing master bedroom with a deep walk-in closet, a large en-suite bathroom that included a walk in shower, a sunken bath and his and hers wash basins with luxury tiles and lighting on the walls and porcelain black tiles on the floor. Patio doors from the bedroom led to a large square balcony that overlooked the trees at the back of the house.

A well-equipped laundry room was also upstairs, to save me the effort of carrying laundry downstairs to the basement. At the end of the landing an archway would lead to a room built above a four car heated garage. Part of that room would be an office for us, with our own computers. The rest of the room would be a fully equipped gym with another outside balcony overlooking the beautiful spruce trees that stood tall and wide at the front of the house.

In total, the house would also have three fabulous bathrooms and a washroom down stairs. The basement was big enough with 8ft high ceilings, to develop into another two bedrooms, a bathroom and another living room.

Matthew had spent hours drawing the plans for that house, calling it our dream home and he would not budge on making it smaller or cheaper. I pleaded with him but he was determined to build the house and told me changing the plans was out of the question. He had drawn up the plans and he fully intended building it. Matthew was so stubborn and nothing would get in his way when he wanted something.

Matthew told me I was to arrange to see a lawyer and sue the clinic. I rose from the sofa and walked back upstairs to bed feeling angry, exhausted and nauseous and put my head on my pillow and cried.

It was the early hours of the morning when Matthew came to bed and I was still awake. I had cried most of the night and Matthew got into bed without asking how I was or saying goodnight.

Chapter Forty

Wednesday morning I woke up with swollen sore eyes from crying and with my body already glowing red from the chemo, I looked a mess.

Matthew was very quiet at breakfast and, as he walked out the door to go to work he didn't speak to any of us. I had never seen him like this and I knew he was leaving it up to me to find a lawyer to help me sue the clinic.

Our lives had changed so much since my skiing accident. The atmosphere in the house was horrible, Matthew and I were constantly bickering and Matthew and Jessica couldn't look at each other without falling out.

It was our third wedding anniversary and for the past two years Matthew had made me feel very special, sending me flowers and taking me out to a lovely restaurant for dinner but this time it passed uneventfully. I didn't even get an anniversary card. Matthew just went to work the same as any other day and I stayed in bed trying to cope with the side effects from my chemo.

My emotions were all over the place with the chemotherapy and I was finding every little thing difficult to cope with, so sitting upstairs in Matthew's office scanning the internet for lawyers in Corby, who specialised in medical misdiagnosis was a major task.

Most of the lawyers' websites had the same headings: Medical Malpractice Lawyers with Years of Experience - No Win No Fee - Compensation Claim Settlements and We Can Help with Negligence or Malpractice.

Derek A J Taylor Law Practice caught my eye, his advert was telling me that, if a doctor failed to diagnose or misdiagnosed, he could be considered negligent and you could seek compensation and sue for damages and that they had a proven track record for advocating and winning cases.

I called the phone number on their website and spoke to a very polite receptionist, who assured me they would be able to help me and made an appointment for me to see the lawyer on the Friday morning at eleven o'clock. Feeling quite pleased with myself, I emailed Matthew the details and his reply came back in a two-word sentence: "Well done."

Friday morning Matthew and I took the elevator to the twenty fourth floor of the Sky Tower, a very impressive tower block standing thirty floors high in the heart of the city centre. It was full of professional offices, a couple of private doctors' clinics, a dental practice and the top two floors were penthouse apartments.

Derek Taylor's Law Practice had a massive office, with a large reception area with classy comfy sofas and coffee tables all set in walnut wood, and had the most amazing view over the city from its windows.

Derek Taylor was a man in his fifties. He was very well dressed and sat behind a large walnut desk. Three of the walls were full of shelves holding hundreds of books and the outside wall was one big glass window which made me feel very uncomfortable, as I'm not that keen on heights. Two leather walnut chairs were placed in front of the desk and Mr Taylor invited us to sit down and asked how he could help us.

Matthew explained about my misdiagnosis at the Kent Cancer Centre and how we had to go to the Weston Clinic in Phoenix for a second opinion and about the loans Matthew had taken out to pay the Medical bills, thinking our private insurance would pay.

My Taylor was very sympathetic but told us, he couldn't help us. There wasn't enough evidence of malpractice but, Matthew might have a case against the Kent Cancer Centre if I died within the following two years. We were devastated and I burst out crying, trying to argue my case, but he stood firm and said it would be too difficult to prove negligence.

We rode the elevator back down to the ground floor and stepped out on to the city centre sidewalk. I just stood there and cried while Matthew held me in his arms. I was drained from any energy I had and could feel my legs giving way underneath me. I really needed to sit down.

We headed for a café across the street and once again, I told Matthew we had to change our house plans but he was as determined as ever that we would build the big house we had planned.

Chapter Forty One

Saturday morning Mathew had a meeting with the builder and the foundations for our new house were due to be laid the following week. Matthew wanted me to go with him but I couldn't get excited about the house, knowing we had this big debt to pay.

Graeme played soccer on a Saturday morning for a local ex-pat British team, so I was going to have Melissa and Jessica to myself. I planned on making us a nice breakfast and, as it was such a beautiful morning, we were going to have it outside on the deck but, before that, I wanted to have a shower, wash my hair and put some makeup on to make me look less like the pale faced, sick looking person I had become.

It felt good standing under the shower with the warm water running down over my body. Since my chemo certain smells would make me nauseous but the luxury body wash and my expensive coconut shampoo were the only things that still smelled as good as they always had.

I had noticed over the past few day's loose hairs on the shower tray and on my pillow when I was making the bed but I didn't pay much attention to it. That morning when I washed my hair clumps of loose strands were sticking to my hands and, when I rinsed my hair, the shower tray was covered with lots of hair.

I had been told there was a 100% chance that all of my hair would fall out and I told myself that, when it happened, I would not let it freak me out but as I blow dried my lovely long hair into my usual style, I found hair strands were being blown from my head and onto the floor. My hair brush was clogged with hair and, when I looked closer, I had bald patches dotted all over my head.

I could hear Melissa and Jessica calling me to make breakfast but I knew there was something I had to do before I went downstairs. With tears falling down my face, I locked the bathroom door tied my long hair into a loose pony tail and took out the hair scissors and hair trimmers that I used to cut Matthew's hair. With the scissors, I cut my hair to within a half inch of my head and was left holding the long thin pony tail. I looked awful with stumpy patchy hair. I plugged in the hair trimmers and, with a shaking hand, I started at the front and moved it across the top of my head. I now had a broad hairless line across my head so I quickly did the same to the rest of my hair. The towel laid across the washbasin was now covered in dark brown hair and I had only a few patches of hair left, which the hair trimmer hadn't cut so I got my razor that I used to shave my legs, covered my head in soap and shaved the rest of the hair off. It was now smooth and all shiny and the person looking back at me in the mirror didn't look like me.

That was the most traumatic and upsetting thing I have ever had to do, even though it was probably the most practical. I wrapped a dry towel around my head in a turban and carefully applied my makeup, putting more on than I usually would, making sure my eyes were perfectly outlined with eye liner and my lips were covered with glossy lipstick.

I collected all the loose hair and put it into a bag to put in the garbage. I cleaned the bathroom so it looked as good as it had when I first walked in to have my shower. When I opened the bathroom door, Melissa and Jessica were standing in front of me crying and I hugged them both and all three of us sobbed.

If I hadn't been in denial about losing my hair, I would have been more organised and bought something to cover my head but now all I had was a towel so that was panic number two. I couldn't walk around with a towel on my head all day and I certainly wasn't going anywhere without it.

It took me over an hour to take the towel off to show Melissa and Jessica my bald head. They were so sweet. They kept telling me how pretty I looked and asked how I got the three scars I had on the back of my head. I got Jessica to hold a mirror behind me so I could see the scars they were talking about. I had one about an inch and half long and two small half inch ones and I remembered exactly how I got them.

My older brother Chris was only fourteen months old when I was born. It had been a shock to my mum, getting pregnant again when Chris was still a baby of five months old. She didn't want another baby so soon. She had had a difficult birth with my brother and wasn't ready to go through that again.

My mum was in labour with me but she didn't want to go to hospital too soon. She didn't want to be in hospital at all but, after the birth of my brother, she wasn't allowed to have a home delivery so she left it until the very last minute before allowing my dad to call for an ambulance to take her to the maternity hospital and I made my appearance on arrival at the hospital.

I was a mistake and my grandparents insisted Chris stayed with them while mum came to terms with having another baby. Poor Chris didn't know what was going on, being taken from his devoted mother. His grandmother thought he would settle better with her if she didn't mention his mum or the new baby, so when his dad brought him back home after a few weeks and he saw his mum sitting on a chair with a baby in her arms, he was not happy.

My mum and dad thought he would welcome his new baby sister but instead he was jealous and blamed me for being parted from him mum. Mum would feel guilty, even though it wasn't her fault and would try to make up for the few weeks they had been apart, giving him as much attention as possible while I was left to sleep in my pram.

When I turned from a screaming little baby to a toddler crawling about the floor, I became more interesting to Chris and we grew up playing together. We were close to each other but we must have driven our mum mad. One minute we would be playing quietly together on the floor with our toys, and the next we were throwing the toys and tearing each other's hair out. I was a tough little girl but no match for my brother when our fights and games got too rough and the scars on my head were the result of me coming off worse.

I hadn't realised I had those scars on my head. I had never seen them and, with always having a full head of thick hair, they were never seen and nobody ever told me they were there.

I knew my mum had never told my brother what had happened when I was born and, even though there were lots of tears from fighting, as an adult I could now understand why we fought so much as kids and I think I turned out to be a good mistake.

Chapter Forty Two

Losing my hair was just another thing I had to deal with on my cancer journey. It made me feel like I had lost my femininity and I no longer looked attractive.

I had read the leaflets the clinic gave me about the harsh effects the chemotherapy would have on my hair follicles and that it would not grow back until I had finished my treatment so I had to be strong and come to terms with it, even though it made me feel so sad.

Melissa and Jessica tried to cheer me up by turning it into an adventure and, after finding me one of their baseball caps, we headed for the shopping mall.

Walking round the mall was hard. I felt as if I stood out like a sore thumb and that everyone was staring at me knowing I had cancer but the girls were great and led me straight to a shop called Angela's Wig

Boutique. There was a sign in the window saying, "We proudly offer only the highest quality and natural looking wigs available today."

The shop assistant was very helpful and explained all the different hair textures and styles. There was so much choice of styles and colours and, with Melissa and Jessica's help, I tried on so many wigs, each one giving me a different look which made the girls laugh.

We finally left the shop with me wearing a straight shoulder length wig which looked lovely with its red highlights through the brown hair. It was made of real hair that I could wash and style however I wanted to.

It felt strange wearing a wig but, when I walked back through the shopping mall my hair was swinging from side to side with every strand cut to the perfect length and I felt more confident than I had when I walked into the mall wearing a baseball cap.

We called into the department store and an assistant from one of the makeup counters gave me a face make over. She cleansed my face then covered it in a foundation, attached some false eye lashes, outlined my eyes and drew me some eye brows with a dark brown pencil, finishing my eyes off with a shiny bronze eye shadow. My cheeks had a light brush of mulberry blusher and my lips were outlined and coloured in with a deep red lipstick.

For the first time that year, I thought I looked beautiful. I kept catching my reflection in the shop windows and, even though I didn't recognise the person looking back at me, I liked the look it gave me and I couldn't wait for Matthew to see me when he got home from seeing the builder.

Matthew thought I looked stunning and took us all out for a celebration drink in the afternoon, where all five of us sat on high stools around a high table in the sports bar sharing a pitcher of beer. I sat back and felt comfortable while I watched Melissa, Graeme, Jessica and Matthew all commenting on the various sports events that were shown on different TV screens and, for once, my cancer was not the topic of conversation.

I tired very easily that night after having such an eventful day so I went to bed early. I wanted to be asleep for when Matthew came to bed. I felt embarrassed at showing him my bald head and naked face, not that he had never seen me without makeup but he hadn't seen me with no hair. Actually he hadn't even seen me with short hair let alone no hair.

I wasn't asleep when Matthew came to bed so I pretended I was and tucked the duvet up around my head. I lay awake like that all night, scared to move and in the morning when Matthew looked at me, I cried.

Chapter Forty Three

Sunday night and I was to have my first injection of Neulasta. Neulasta was used to increase my white blood cell levels, to help my immune system to work properly as the chemotherapy drugs reduced the levels in my body, which could have made me more prone to infection. It also made sure I was strong enough for my next round of chemotherapy.

My chemo nurse Cathy had given me the pre-filled syringes and shown me how to inject myself and had also given me a leaflet with instructions so I wouldn't forget. Sitting on the bed I read the leaflet about six times but my hands were shaking so much I couldn't inject myself.

Melissa would have been the perfect person to give me the injection but she went out to the movies with Graeme so Matthew had to do it. Cathy did warn me that it could sting, as the drug had to be injected slowly into the stomach.

Every time Matthew came near me with the injection, I moved, so he made me lie still on my back on the bed and, with my face hidden under the pillow, he gave me the injection under the skin in my stomach. It seemed to take ages to go in and it really stung. I don't know how he did it with me screeching at him.

The next morning I couldn't move. Every bone in my body was screaming out to me in pain. It felt like my body was being destroyed rather than rebuilding blood cells.

I spent all day in bed feeling miserable and, when my mum called, I once again broke down crying on the phone to her.

The pain had passed by the next day and I was left with fatigue from both my chemo and the injection and I didn't look forward to repeating this after my next round of chemo.

When Melissa parked the car in the underground parking lot for my fifth week of treatment I had to hold my nose and walk as fast as I could into the entrance of the clinic.

The smell of the petrol fumes coming from the cars was making me feel sick and, when I passed a very well dressed lady in the corridor, I could smell her strong perfume and I had to run into the ladies toilet to vomit and that was before I even got to the chemo unit.

Jamie was back in the bed next to me but this time he was not looking very well and his dad stayed with him throughout the day while he had his treatment.

Those chemo sessions were so exhausting and this one seemed to affect me more quickly than the previous ones. After vomiting in the toilets I was vomiting again shortly after the first chemo drug, Adriamycin, started going through my veins. This treatment was getting harder and I didn't even know if it was doing me any good. I felt it was taking the life out of me instead of saving my life.

Tuesday and Wednesday I was once again written off with me in bed feeling ill. I went to the bathroom in the middle of Tuesday night to be sick and I was so exhausted that I fell asleep on the rug on the bathroom floor.

Thursday was Jessica's prom night at school. She had done very well in the two years she had been there and got good grades in her exams. I was so proud of her. Before I started treatment I took Jessica to buy her prom outfit and she chose a beautiful royal blue long satin prom dress with a mermaid silhouette, sweetheart neckline with beading across the top and down one side of the dress. It was a beautiful dress and she looked stunning in it.

Parents and family had tickets to attend the award ceremony and the prom dance for the students was to follow after it. I was so sick that night it was impossible for me to go and I cried as I helped Jessica into her dress. Her hair was gathered up and pinned on top of her head with curly strands falling down the sides of her face. Her makeup was perfect and she looked beautiful as she twirled around the floor in the living room showing off her new look. I felt happy for Jessica but sad for missing out and, when Jessica, Matthew, Melissa and Graeme got into Matthew's truck and drove down the road, I cried so much. Cancer had once again stood in the way of a major family event and nobody knew how much it hurt me not seeing my beautiful daughter walk tall and proud onto the stage to receive her high school certificates. The feeling of letting her down weighed heavily on me and I knew I would never get that night back.

Chapter Forty Four

We had a big weekend ahead of us. The sale of our house was to complete on the Friday and we would be moving into the apartment we had rented in the city.

I had very little energy and packing up the house into storage boxes was a nightmare. One by one every kitchen item, every ornament and every personal item was all wrapped and placed into boxes. It was such a big task for me. Only two years ago I was doing the same thing in the UK for our move to Canada and now we were on the move again.

For two years we all enjoyed living in such a beautiful house, a house we could never have afforded back in the UK. We all enjoyed our family life that surrounded the house and together we went through the adjustment of emigrating and settling in Canada.

I loved my family and I loved us all living together. Matthew had big dreams since he came to Canada and not just to design and build us a new dream home. He wanted his own business, a holiday cabin on a lake, a fishing boat, canoes, quad bikes and every other gadget the Canadian culture had to offer but I was happy with what we had. I wasn't ready for moving on just yet, I had settled where we were and now with me having cancer I didn't want my surroundings to change and I couldn't see as far into the future as Matthew could.

They say moving is one of the most stressful things you can do in life. Well, add that to going through chemo, treatment and being stressed doesn't begin to describe how I was felling. This new house was becoming a nightmare to me.

Most of our belongings were going into storage and the rest was going to the apartment so Matthew was carefully placing boxes in order on the drive so the removal men would know which was going where.

What hurt me the most was that we had come to the end of all living together. Melissa and Graeme had rented a lovely two bedroom split-level apartment south of the city and had moved into it a couple of days previously.

With the last item and box loaded into the removal van, they drove down the street with all our belongings with Matthew following in his truck.

Jessica and I were left in the empty house and we sat on the living room floor with our backs up against the wall. Neither of us wanted this move and we felt so sad.

We were about to leave when our neighbour came over to us with a box of biscuits and wished us good luck. We were shocked. We hadn't spoken to her since the argument we had when we got back from Phoenix. This was the first time she had been nice towards us since we moved in. She was probably glad to see the back of us and I certainly hoped I wouldn't have another neighbour like her.

Our apartment was number 1604 on the sixteenth floor and it seemed to take ages for the elevator to get there. The apartment had a small hall that led into a small kitchen with basic kitchen cabinets and cooker and an area to put a table and chairs, where we had to put our garden furniture because we had given our pine round kitchen table and chairs to Melissa and Graeme for their new place.

The living room was a nice size, with a full glass wall with patio doors leading out onto a balcony and the view was amazing, overlooking the river with the high level bridge in the middle that led the way into the centre of downtown Corby with the sky scraper buildings towering above. The view fascinated me but being afraid of heights made it scary for me to go outside and stand on the balcony.

It had two good-sized bedrooms but only one bathroom that we were going to have to share with Jessica.

After living in such a big house this apartment felt very small and we only had a minimum amount of furniture that we brought with us so Jessica and I had our work cut out to make it look nice.

That was such a busy day and, by early evening, I was so exhausted I didn't want anything to eat and collapsed on the sofa and went into a deep sleep then woke up forgetting where I was.

At first I found it a novelty living sixteen floors above everything, I could sit on the sofa and look out over the city and, at night, the view was amazing with all the buildings lit up in different colours and I loved to watch the lights from the traffic down below.

There were lovely walking trails along the river and, on my good days, I would take the elevator down to the ground floor and walk out of the main entrance across the road and down a few steps and I was on the trails, which were lined with trees on one side and open to the river on the other.

There were benches along the grass verge and I had my favourite one, set into the riverbank amongst the bushes and shrubs and

I would stop at it and sit and look across the river to the oldest building in Corby.

Unlike the UK where buildings can be hundreds of years old, the oldest building here was a Chateau-style hotel that was built in 1912 and owned by the Canadian National Railway. Prior to the hotel being constructed in 1915 the site was home to a squatters' camp. The squatters often lived in tents or in small caves dug into the side of the river valley wall. They say many of the squatters were Ukrainian-speaking immigrants from the Austro-Hungarian province of Galicia.

I would sit on the bench and close my eyes trying to see the images from those early days and wonder how they coped living in tents and caves when the temperature would drop thirty or forty below in the winter.

On the trail people would ride their bikes past me while others were balancing on roller blades or skate boards and I used to wonder who they were and where were they going and whether any of them had cancer like me. Was

I the only one on the trail that was battling this dreadful disease?

Jessica didn't settle very well in the apartment and I felt so sorry for her. She had struggled with moving away from her friends in the UK and now we were moving her away from her new friends. They were now twenty kilometres away and Jessica didn't drive so she depended on me driving her to meet up with them.

She came home one night with a new boyfriend, a nineteen year old boy called Derek. He lived on the other side of the river in a part of the city I didn't know. He was nice enough if a bit shy and he couldn't understand a word we said, what with Matthews Scottish accent and our English slang.

He would wear the craziest brightly coloured clothes and, when Jessica brought him to the apartment to meet us, Matthew and I had a hard job trying not to laugh at his bright yellow baggy trousers, orange t-shirt and dark, thick, wild, bushy, curly hair. I think he was keener on Jessica than she was on him so it didn't last very long.

Jessica was offered a job in a hair salon as an apprentice hair stylist something she really wanted to have a career in. The problem was it was back in the town from where we had just moved.

Jessica desperately wanted to accept the job and it was too far for me to keep driving her to and from work so she arranged to live with her friend's parents while she was at work through the week and come home on her days off. However, this didn't work out and Jessica found a furnished basement in a bungalow that she rented from an elderly lady.

It broke my heart the day I drove her belongings over to that house and saw the dingy, cold, dark rooms of the basement. It only had small narrow windows so there was not much light.

Her bedroom was small, with a double bed under the narrow window and a single wardrobe and a set of drawers on another wall, only giving her a small area to walk in. The bathroom had a shower, wash basin and toilet crammed into another small space. It did have a sitting area with an old rugged sofa and coffee table but, again, not much light. I'm not even sure Jessica was happy there, but she never said anything.

My children had all moved out now and I felt sad. They hadn't gone by choice. It was our fault for selling the lovely family house. It didn't bother Matthew. He was quite pleased to have me to himself but I missed the girls and Graeme.

After years of running after the three of them, doing everything for them, making their breakfasts, tidying up after them and making dinner for them coming home in the evening, I missed them so much. No more was there the buzz of noise while everyone caught up on their day's events and, when Matthew left to go to work, I would feel I had no reason to get out of bed.

Melissa would come and pick me up to take me to the clinic for my chemotherapy and appointments but it wasn't the same and my bad days after chemo were spent in the apartment on my own.

I missed Melissa and Jessica popping into the bedroom checking I was ok. I had never lived in a house without my children and it was hard. I missed them and needed them so much.

Chapter Forty Five

It was now the middle of July and I was coming towards the end of my second cycle of chemo. I had been through eight weeks of this now, with four sessions of chemo. My eyelashes and eyebrows had vanished and I was bald all over and the only good thing about that was I didn't have to shave my legs every morning in the shower or spend ages drying my hair.

It was so hot outside that wearing my wig would make my head sweat and itch so I didn't wear it in the apartment and, when I went outside, I wore a sun hat or a bandana.

In the beginning, I had chronic indigestion and now I would get quite a few upset stomachs. Sometimes I used to wonder if this, was really happening to me and ended up with a kind of feeling sorry for myself depression and would cry over anything.

At one of my appointments with Dr Wheeldon I sat in front of him and asked, "Why me?" his answer shocked me when he said, "Why not you? You are stronger and fitter than some of my other patients." I certainly didn't feel strong, let alone fit. He said I had to keep going and fight with all the strength I had to overcome the disease.

He told me a cancer support service was available and offered to book me in with a cancer counsellor but I refused. I knew I had to do this myself. I wasn't very good at pouring my heart out to strangers.

Later that day I was very restless and went to bed. I was lying face down, crying into the pillow and feeling sorry for myself, when I felt someone tap me on my shoulder. When I turned round, I saw my dad sitting on the bed next to me. He held my hand, looked straight into my eyes and spoke to me in a firm voice, telling me to stop crying, that he had raised me to be a tough girl and I had to have hope, to be strong and remember I was loved and never ever to give up. I opened my mouth to speak but he was gone. Was it a dream or did I just imagine he was there or did he really come as a spirit, knowing I needed him?

I believed that he came because I needed him and his words made me realise that I had to start fighting this cancer and not let it knock me any further down.

I stopped crying and got out of bed, had a shower then covered my body with body lotion and put on my favourite flowery summer dress. I made a note to ask Mellissa to buy me some false eye lashes, as my eyes looked a bit strange without any, and tied a pretty scarf around my head. Then I looked in the mirror and thought, "stay positive and you'll get through this."

When Matthew came home from work he walked into the apartment hearing soft music playing, a light breeze blowing through the open patio doors and the table set out with a nice summer salad and salmon and an opened bottle of chardonnay in the wine cooler but, most of all, he found me greeting him with a smile.

Since we had moved into the apartment I had had no time for Matthew or any interest in our new house that was being built. I had even refused to go with him on a weekend to see how the house was progressing so Matthew had stopped talking about it. Actually he had stopped talking about most things.

He stopped coming home at his normal time of 5 o'clock and would work on until late in the evening and, when he did come home, I would be lying in bed not feeling very well after chemo and he would find his dinner in the fridge on a plate.

He would spend the rest of the evening doing work on his computer and, by the time he came to bed, which was normally after midnight, I would be fast asleep and if, I wasn't asleep, I would pretend I was.

I relied on Melissa for support. She was the one who would take me for all my clinic appointments and would phone me twice a day to check I was ok.

Matthew and I seemed to be going down a path of not enjoying life together and I felt I was the one that had to pull it back. My dad was right. I had to fight this cancer and stop letting it drag me down and I had to stop pushing Matthew away and he had to start being a bit more caring.

That evening, we had a long talk to try and sort out our problems. Matthew listened when I told him how low I had been feeling and how much I missed the girls and Graeme and I listened when he told me he didn't know how to deal with me being sick which was why he threw himself into his work and the new house. He told me he had been battling with our local health authority and got them to agree to pay for most of my treatment in Phoenix and I felt bad that, with everything that had gone on, I had forgotten about the outstanding loans.

Chapter Forty Six

The weekend before my next chemotherapy treatment I was feeling fit enough for a walk and, instead of walking down the river valley trails by myself, Matthew and I walked from the apartment to Park Avenue. It wasn't very far and, being another beautiful day, it was nice to be out in the warm sunshine.

After calling into Café Connect for a coffee and club sandwich we walked to Paddy's Irish Bar and Matthew introduced me to Ricky and his wife Barbara. Ricky had just joined the company Matthew worked for and, although they were from Aberdeen in Scotland, they had moved to Corby from Jakarta where he had been working.

I took to Ricky and Barbara right away. They were around the same age as us and it was nice to talk to someone from back in the UK. Barbara was an attractive woman with long black hair that fell down her back and with her strong Scottish accent, I could imagine her dressed in a kilt with a heavy shawl wrapped around her shoulders walking through the heather on a misty morning in the highlands of Scotland. She had a fantastic personality, very friendly and fun to be with.

She had an infectious laugh and, for the first time in a long time, she would make me laugh until I cried and my cancer was pushed to one side. I didn't even know if they knew I had cancer because it never came up in conversation.

I found out that Ricky and Barbara were renting an apartment just along the river from ours and, when we all walked home from the Irish bar together, they invited us in for a drink. Their apartment was newer than ours and only on the fourth floor so sitting on the balcony was more appealing to me than our balcony sixteen floors up. They had interesting furniture, with lots of traditional pieces that they had bought in Jakarta, such as a dark carved wooden coffee table and wooden carved figures. In the dining area stood a fabulous round heavy dark wooden table with four carved wooden chairs placed around it where we all sat and shared a few glasses of wine. Ricky had a large collection of guitars in one of the bedrooms and was proud to show them off and play for us.

For the first time in the two years since we had moved to Canada, I felt I had found a girl friend, something that had been missing from my life for too long so when a couple of days after we met in the Irish bar Barbara called me and invited me to go to her place for a coffee, I didn't hesitate in saying yes and just after lunch I walked the short distance to her apartment.

Barbara was so welcoming and her apartment had a lovely aroma of fresh coffee. She sat me down on the comfy sofa and poured two cups of coffee and placed them on the coffee table in front of me with a plate of homemade gingerbread.

Sitting opposite me in a vintage antique wooden armchair with deep rusty red cushions, she told me she knew about my cancer and asked me if she could talk to me about it.

I was shocked Barbara was the first person I had come across outside my family who didn't respond strangely to my cancer. When you have cancer it consumes every thinking moment you have and it's very hard to focus on anything else. I found at home with my family the first thing they would ask me was, how was I feeling, which would lead me into saying how rotten I felt or I would just brush over it and say I was fine and they would know not to talk about it any further.

I found other people had no idea what to say to me so they never mentioned it, probably because they were frightened they might upset me. Some people saw it as my death sentence and they were glad it wasn't happening to them so they would avoid any eye contact with me. This happened to me one afternoon when Matthew and I met Melissa and Graeme in a sports bar for lunch and their friends came over to the table to say hello. I knew all of them, they had been to our house several times and I had always had a good chat with them, but that day they stood by our table for over ten minutes chatting and they never once looked my way not even saying hello to me. I asked Mellissa after they had gone why they hadn't spoken to me and her reply was that they knew I had cancer and thought I was dying so they didn't know what to say to me.

I was also being ignored by my good friend Jackie who, I had known for years. She used to call me every few weeks to catch up but since she got the news I had cancer, she stopped ringing me. I tried to call her a few times but her husband would say she was out shopping or something. I didn't blame her or anyone else for reacting the way they did but I did wish they would have been brave enough to ask me how I was. I just wished they would treat me normally.

Barbara talked freely to me, asking questions. She asked me how I was coping with the side effects from the chemo and about the psychological and emotional side effects of having cancer. She also wanted to know how I was coping with the way my family was coping.

She was such a lovely caring person, I found it easy to talk to her and was able to be honest about the way I was feeling and it was good to talk about my family. I guess this is what counselling is like but I didn't see it as counselling, I just saw it as girl friend talk.

After a couple of hours of pouring my heart out to her and shedding a few tears, she opened a nice bottle of Australian red wine and we sat outside on the wicker chairs on the balcony feeling the heat of the sun. We drank the whole bottle of wine while people watching and laughing like two best friends.

Barbara had so many interesting stories to tell, as she had lived all around the world while Ricky moved from one oil company to another, giving them his expertise in engineering.

She had two sons. Her youngest, David, had stayed in Jakarta as he was still in university and her older son James was married and living back in her home town of Aberdeen in

Scotland, where Barbara and Ricky intended to return when they retired.

They say people come into your life for a reason and I believed Barbara came into mine when I needed her the most. Having cancer made me feel like I was living in a lonely bubble where nobody fully understood my life and that nothing was ever going to be normal.

I would worry that my cancer treatment would not work, that 2000 was going to be the year I would die and that I would only be remembered by people as Lisa Wright the woman who emigrated to Canada and died of cancer.

That afternoon Barbara brought me back to feeling normal. Having her as my friend, I knew I could turn to her with my troubles and I knew she would be there for me.

Chapter Forty Seven

Monday 17th July I was starting my third cycle of chemotherapy and, even though a couple of days before Barbara had lifted me, I was now back down, dreading the day ahead of me.

On the day unit Jamie was not in the bed next to me and, when I asked Cathy where he was, she told me he was not coming back for any more treatment. I knew that was bad news for Jamie so, as the poison ran through my veins attacking the cancer cells on its way, I began to cry.

I was crying not only for Jamie but also for myself, I was frightened and started wondering how many of us who were on the unit that day would live to tell the tale of their cancer journey.

I got so upset Cathy had to sedate me for the rest of the day while I had my chemotherapy and Melissa sat by my bedside waiting for my treatment to finish so she could take me home and tuck me back up in bed.

That night, Melissa stayed over at the apartment. She was worried about me and wanting to be there for me and to give support to Matthew, who didn't really know how to deal with me being so upset.

The week that followed I felt dreadful. I didn't want to get out of bed and I certainly didn't want to talk to anyone so my mum's phone calls once again went to the answer machine.

I seemed to be vomiting more, every bone and muscle in my body seemed to ache, I had a very sore throat and a croaky voice, I was soaked in sweat and was shivering all over unable to get warm.

Matthew took my temperature and it was reading 38.7c so he phoned the oncology help line at the hospital. The nurse on the other end of the phone told Matthew my temperature was in what they called a "danger zone" and, with my immune system being at an all-time low, any infection could take hold very quickly.

Having a high temperature is the first sign there is something wrong and, if it was an infection, I needed to be treated right away so it didn't develop into anything more serious.

Weeks ago, when I first attended the day unit, Cathy gave me a prescription for some antibiotics which I was told to keep in my medicine cabinet in case I needed them. The nurse was telling Matthew to start giving me the antibiotics every four hours and to give me some Tylenol to help reduce the fever and he was to make sure he got lots of fluids into me so I didn't get dehydrated.

The nurse also told him he was to take my temperature again in an hour and call her back with the reading.

Matthew phoned his boss and told him he would not be going into work that day. An hour later, he took my temperature and it was down to 38.3c. He reported this to the nurse who said she would call him back again in another hour. Half an hour later, the phone rang and Matthew was told to take me straight to the oncology department at the clinic, where I would be seen by a doctor.

It took all my energy to get out of bed and put my clothes on and, when I was ready, Matthew strapped me into the passenger seat of his truck and drove me to the Kent Cancer Centre.

When we got there we were lead into a small room, where the nurse took some vials of blood, hooked up to a saline drip to put some fluids into me, then gave me an injection of antibiotics.

I slept on and off all day while the nurses constantly checked my temperature and kept giving me antibiotic injections and Tylenol. By the evening my temperature had dropped back to a normal reading. A doctor I hadn't seen before came to see me and told me the blood tests showed I didn't have an infection and it was probably just a cold and I could go home as long as I keep taking the Tylenol every four hours and continued with the antibiotics.

He told me a cold can be serious when your immune system is so low. It can develop into a chest infection and that would warrant a stay in hospital until it cleared up and it would delay my next chemo.

I was glad to be back in my own bed and Matthew kept a close eye on me to make sure my cold didn't develop further.

Having a cold had me wiped out and my so called good week ended up not being so good. I finally got out of bed on the Friday.

After not taking my mums phone calls all week, I phoned her for a long chat and told her what had happened. My poor mum she was having a hard time being so far away from me back in England but I still wouldn't let her come over. I knew how upsetting it would be for her to see me with no hair, vomiting after treatment and looking so pale and weak. Maybe I was protecting her from that upset or maybe I was being selfish because I knew she would have pity and concern in her eyes and she would fuss over me and cry herself to sleep at night worrying about me and I couldn't cope with that.

I was having a tough time with my emotions all over the place and I knew I would end up getting angry with her and we would fall out and that was the last thing I wanted to do to her.

Chapter Forty Eight

Monday 14th August 7.30am and as I opened the patio doors to the balcony I could feel the heat from the morning sun flooding through the apartment. As the sun was rising up into the sky it lit shadows across the river and the city, and the tall office block windows were reflecting the sun.

It was the start of rush hour and people were driving over the high level bridge to work while others were enjoying their morning walk before the start of a busy day.

Today was to be my last session of chemo and, while I waited for Melissa to arrive, I gathered together a big box of Quality Street I had bought from Safeway and the bunch of yellow roses I had got from a lovey florist at the top of Park Avenue.

It was the usual routine, weight and blood pressure checked then I got my blood taken and I had to wait in the waiting room for the results before I could go onto the day unit. Melissa kept me from being bored and one of the nurses brought us a cup of coffee each while we waited.

Dr Wheeldon finally called us into his room and I couldn't stop myself from saying how pleased I was that today was the last lot of chemo I would have but Dr Wheeldon wiped the smile from my face when he told me my platelets had taken a nose dive and the count was too low for me to have my treatment.

I didn't know what platelets were until he explained they are tiny cells that help the blood to clot. Made in large numbers by the bone marrow, each platelet develops in the bone marrow and is then released into the bloodstream where it circulates around the body through the veins and arteries.

When a blood vessel is damaged the platelets will travel to the injured site and clump together to form a clot. If they drop too low there's a higher risk of bleeding and sometimes a platelet transfusion is necessary to stop them getting so low.

Dr Wheeldon told me I had to go back on Friday to get my bloods checked again and, if everything was ok, I could have my chemotherapy the following Monday.

I walked out of his room in floods of tears. Even Melissa had tears in her eyes, I was so disappointed. I just wanted to complete my last session, knowing that the chemo was coming to an end, but now it was going to drag on to another week and I felt like a football player in a cup final game when the final whistle is about to blow and you're told you have to go into extra time.

With Matthew injecting me into my stomach three nights in a row with Filgrastin my white cell count was back up by Monday morning and I once again walked into the day unit where Cathy gave me a big hug when I handed her the flowers and gave her the Quality Street to share.

Four months I had been going to that unit and, as I looked around the room at the patients hooked up to their IV bags of toxic fluids, I thought about how I had seen so many of them come and go.

I looked towards Jamie's bed and hoped he was ok. There was someone new in his bed, an elderly lady with grey curly hair, who was telling the patient in the bed next to her about her cancer and that this was the first day of her treatment. I felt sad for her, knowing what she was going to have to go through.

I looked at the nurses with their happy smiley faces. They never stopped running from one end of that unit to another, always having time to help, to comfort and to listen to the patients.

Then I looked at Melissa and thought, what would I have done without her. I don't think I could have gone through those long days lying in bed feeling sicker as one chemo drug after another was pumped through my veins. She would wipe my face with a warm face cloth, hold my hand and hug me when I cried.

Every week my daughter had sat next to my bed for eight hours, going through every minute of my chemo treatment with me and today should have been the first day in her new job as an Emergency Medical Technician for the City Ambulance Service. Instead she had asked them if she could delay her start date until the Wednesday so she could take me for my treatment. I don't think she had any idea how much it meant to me that she was there for me and I couldn't have loved her more.

As we walked out of the unit at 5 o'clock, all the nurses hugged us and wished me well and wished Melissa good luck in her new job. I was in floods of tears thinking I could never thank those oncology chemotherapy nurses enough. They were a very special breed of nurses and I think some of the most wonderful people on this earth. I don't think they realise what an important role they play and what a difference they make to the lives of us cancer patients, or how much we count on them to help get us through the trauma of chemotherapy.

Chapter Forty Nine

I now had a few weeks' break from treatment; no more chemotherapy, no more injections in the stomach and hopefully no more vomiting.

My radiation therapy was not due to start until 18th September so I was looking forward to catching up with Ricky and Barbara in the Irish bar and most of all having some fun times with my family.

The first week I spent in bed dealing with the side effects from my last chemo and the second week I had an appointment for a CT scan so they could see how well the treatment had gone and to determine how much radiation therapy I was to have.

I couldn't sleep the night before my scan. So many things were going through my head.

It had been a tough year so far and my weekly chemo visits and weeks of suffering the side effects were now going to be questioned. Had it all been worth it?

It was 9.30am when I walked into the radiology department, feeling very nervous, with my stomach churning. I had been told I wasn't to eat or drink anything after midnight the night before and my lips were feeling dry, not to mention the sticky dry feeling in my mouth.

I didn't have anyone with me, Matthew had a very important business meeting and Mellissa was at work.

I was called into another room and, after changing into a hospital gown, I was seated alongside two other people; one was an elderly man who smiled at me when I sat down and the other was a lady who I would say was in her fifties. She looked up at me then looked straight back down and carried on reading the magazine she had in her hands.

A nurse called me into a small cubicle and, after searching the back of both my hands for a decent vein she poked a needle in and inserted a cannula. When I had sat down next to the elderly man the nurse gave me an empty glass and not one but two big jugs of fluid. She told me it was a barium sulphate suspension and I had to drink every last drop. Being thirsty, I didn't think that was going to be a problem but was I in for a shock. It tasted like a very thin chalky banana milk shake. It was not very nice and quite difficult to swallow. The nurse told me to take my time because I had ninety minutes in which to drink it.

She pointed across the room to a row of three toilets and told me I was to use the one on the right. I was beginning to think this was not going to be a very pleasant experience and I was right.

Fifteen minutes in and I was starting to feel queasy and I needed to go to the toilet. I had diarrhoea and the smell was foul which just made me want to vomit more. When I finally came out of the toilet the nurse came over to me and told me I wasn't allowed to vomit because vomiting up a substantial quantity of the suspension could void the effects on the

CT scan and produce unusable results, which would result in a retest.

An awful ninety minutes later the jugs were empty and I was feeling very weak and looked as white as a sheet. I was desperate to vomit every last drop of this fluid out of my stomach.

The nurse called me into the x-ray room and I couldn't believe it when she handed me a small plastic cup full of the fluid I had just taken ninety minutes to drink and told me to quickly drink it. Then they would get started. That last cup was so hard to get down and even harder to keep down.

Thankfully the scan itself didn't take too long and, as soon as it was over, I headed straight for the toilet where on my knees leaning over the toilet, I vomited every last drop out of my stomach and that was one scan I hoped would never have to be repeated.

Chapter Fifty

Sitting in Dr Wheeldon's treatment room a few days later, he told me the results of the scan. It showed that the chemotherapy treatment had done its job and shrunk part of the tumour and, as he spoke, I could feel my shoulders drop and my body relax. This was encouraging news but Dr Wheeldon then told me, as much as it was good news he would have expected the chemotherapy to have shrunk more of the tumour than it had and he was going to start my radiotherapy on the 18th September.

Dr Wheeldon was very good and explained in depth the next stage of my fight, saying that radiotherapy uses high energy particles to destroy cancer cells.

A carefully focused beam of radiation would be delivered from a machine to my body, after the radiation team had taken careful measurements to determine the dose needed and the correct angles for aiming the radiation beams.

I was to have extended field radiation given to my mediastinum area where my tumour was, as well as the surrounding "normal" lymph node areas just in case the Hodgkin's disease had spread, even though they could not detect it in these areas.

I was to have the treatment in two cycles starting Monday the 18th September, both being over a four week period and I was to have it every day between Monday to Friday with a month off in between.

The first month of radiation was to be given to the lymph node area in my neck, chest and upper arms and the second cycle would hit the lymph nodes in my upper abdomen, spleen and pelvis.

This treatment also came with short and long term side effects, the short ones being feeling tired, nausea, dry mouth and diarrhoea, all sounding similar to the side effects from the chemo. The long term ones were a bit scarier, with an increased risk of another cancer in the parts of the body that had been exposed to the radiation, damage to the thyroid gland, increased risk of heart failure and stroke and damage to my ovaries.

Dr Wheeldon said they would try and reduce these long term risks by aiming the radiation beam as accurately as possible and by placing shields over nearby parts of my body to protect them. I didn't want to think about the long term side effect. All I wanted was for it to kill the rest of the cancer cells and give me my life back.

Chapter Fifty One

It was the middle of the afternoon by the time I got back to the apartment and the only words that stayed in my head from seeing Dr Wheeldon was that I didn't need any more chemo and part of the tumour had vanished. I was thrilled with this news and, for the first time in eight months, I had some good news to tell everyone.

The first thing I did was lift the phone out of the cradle and dial the number for Matthew's office, knowing he would be so pleased with my news, but when he answered I didn't get past saying "hello" when he told me he was late for a meeting and would talk to me that night when he got home. I was hurt. It would have only taken two minutes for me to tell him my news. He knew I was going to see Dr Wheeldon for results.

I wanted to phone my mum, my brothers and my friends but, with the time difference of seven hours behind in England, mum would be in bed. She never liked anyone phoning her after nine o'clock and it was too late to phone anyone else. Jessica was at work and so was Mellissa and Graeme so the only person left to call was my new friend Barbara but that went straight to voice mail.

Sitting on the sofa looking out of the open patio window at the blue sky, I now felt so alone. For the first time since arriving in Canada, I now felt a million miles away from everything that was familiar and safe and I wasn't quite sure that this was where I wanted to be.

It had been exciting when we first moved here, like being on one long holiday, exploring and discovering new things together and I was happy until we sold the house and the girls and Graeme moved out.

Matthew was always at work and, when he was at home, he was back to sitting at his computer, working until the early hours of the morning or, after work, he would drive out to check on how the progress of the new house was coming on.

Melissa would pop in on her days off and I would drive for an hour to visit Jessica if I was having a good day after my treatment.

I had no friends other than Barbara, I missed all my old friends back in England. Truth be told, I missed my old life style. I never ever felt alone back there, someone was always calling round for a chat over a cup of coffee while we planned our next night out or dates for the next house party or just caught up on the local gossip.

I missed my old job and the fun I had with the eight girls and two doctors I worked with at the medical practice, and not forgetting my running club friends. Every one of those friends and work colleagues would be there for me today, now I longed for that life again.

Matthew's and my relationship had changed. Back then, we would work all week and the Friday would be the start of our weekend, meeting friends for drinks after work, going to a party on the Saturday night and spending all Sunday outdoors.

Matthew and I were always laughing, always planning our next holiday or weekend away. We'd cuddle up together in bed and wake feeling happy.

Now we hardly talked and we never went to bed at the same time so cuddling up together never happened.

I knew Matthew's job was demanding and he probably felt he had a lot to prove so work was constantly on his mind. The new house had become his project and every bit of spare time he had was spent up there chatting and checking on the builders.

My cancer had also changed things between us. After the intense trip to Phoenix, Matthew seemed to have taken a step back and let Mellissa take the support roll in taking care of me.

I seemed to have a husband who provided, not the husband who was my best friend and soul mate. We were not even lovers any more. I didn't think he found me attractive any more.

Losing my hair and being sick had probably paid the price for that.

Nobody would know how strong that overwhelming feeling of loneliness was, nor would they see me cry for the life I wanted back. If they had I would see that as a sign of weakness and I hated being weak.

I was so home sick I wanted to book a flight home. I wanted to see my mum and see my friends. I longed to feel the rain on my face. I never thought I would miss the British weather but I did. So, on the day I should have been feeling happy, I was feeling so sad.

In the weeks leading up to my radiotherapy I tried my best to snap out of that homesick feeling. I searched through recipe books and made some exciting dinners for Matthew and me, I made more of an effort with my makeup and bought some new clothes. I went shopping for things for the new house and I would be all enthusiastic about them when Matthew came home from work.

One morning after having a shower, I was smoothing moisturising cream into my face when I noticed a dark shadow all over my head and, when I looked closer, it was my hair growing back. When I ran my hand over my head I could feel the soft spiky hair sprouting out all over. I was finally getting my hair back.

I was so excited that I jumped back into the shower and washed what hair was there with shampoo. There was hardly enough to warrant washing it but it was something I just had to do. Losing my hair had been one of the hardest things to accept.

Every day I noticed it grow a little bit more and I would sit outside on the apartment balcony as close as possible to the open patio door. With my fear of heights I wasn't brave enough to move closer to the rail. I would sit there and let the sun beat down on my head, hoping it would help my hair grow faster.

Those couple of weeks flew by and I was starting to feel as if I had more energy and, not only was the hair on my head growing back, my eye lashes and eye brows had also returned and, for the first time in months, I was able to wear mascara.

Chapter Fifty Two

Monday 18th September and my first radiotherapy session was at 10 o'clock. I had to go by myself as Matthew was too busy at work to go with me and Melissa was working. Not that I would have asked her to come along with me. She had done her share when I was going through my chemo and it was time for her to have a break.

It had been a month since I had last been at the Kent Cancer Centre and, to be honest, I had forgotten what Dr Wheeldon had said about the radiotherapy, other than I had to come every day at the same time.

I followed the signs for the radiotherapy department and, after walking through several corridors, I entered the reception area and booked in for my appointment.

After changing into a hospital gown, I was shown into a room with a huge machine in the middle of it. The radiographer called it a simulator and it was hovering over the bed I was to be lying on. The shields they had made to protect parts of my body were gently placed on me then the radiographer drew marks on my skin where they were going to be aiming the beam of radiation.

I was told it would not take long and I had to stay as still as possible as the simulator moved over my body, doing its job. After the front had been done I had to lie on my stomach and the same was done on my upper back and neck. The whole procedure only took minutes and I never felt a thing. I was dressed and back in my car on my way home before I knew it.

I returned the next day and the day after that and I was beginning to think this part of my treatment was going to be easy but, after Thursday's session, my skin had become red, dry and itchy and it looked darker, with a tinge of blue and black, and felt sore and flaky. The radiographer told me not to use perfumed soaps, talcum powder, deodorant, creams or lotions and to have showers instead of baths.

She told me Dr Wheeldon would prescribe me some cream if my skin got worse.

That night, when I went in the shower, I could not stand the spray of the water hitting my body and the next day I was back to feeling exhausted, another side effect that would probably last throughout all the treatment.

I developed burns to my skin, especially on my neck, and they would blister and be very painful. My throat was constantly sore with mouth ulcers and I lost my taste buds. These side effects were much worse than the chemotherapy side effects and Dr Wheeldon prescribed me mouth washes, gels and creams.

What upset me most was that the radiation which had been blasting away at the lymph nodes on my neck had destroyed the hair follicles half way up my head and all the new hair that had grown back was now dead and had fallen out. I looked awful. The hair on top of my head was still growing and now a good half inch long. I had to wear my wig again because I didn't want to shave off the top hair and be bald again and I was told it could take months before the hair would grow back due to the damage to the follicles.

This treatment was so brutal I decided to tell Dr Wheeldon I couldn't take any more of it. I never told Matthew or the girls that I was going to stop my treatment as I didn't want them to be upset, instead intending to make up some story telling them that Dr Wheeldon said it wasn't necessary to continue the treatment because it had already done its job.

The morning I arrived for my appointment with Dr Wheeldon I was all fired up ready with my speech in my head and I wasn't going to be talked out of it.

When I walked into the waiting area I saw it was full of patients waiting to be seen and I knew I was in for a long wait. Then I saw Jamie, the beautiful young man from the chemo unit. I was thrilled to see him and we hugged each other very tightly.

He confirmed the doctor was running about an hour behind and he had already been waiting for over half an hour. He looked pale and thin and told me he only had another two weeks of radiotherapy until his treatment was complete. We swopped stories about the side effects and how we were both finding it tough going.

He told me his big plans for going back to college to do the year he had just missed and how he had fallen for a girl he knew and was going to ask her out when he got his strength back. He also told me it was his twentieth birthday in two days.

When Jamie was called for his appointment, I knew there were still a few people to be seen in front of me so I quickly went to the little shop I had passed in the corridor on my way in and bought Jamie a birthday card.

Back in my seat in the waiting room, I waited for Jamie to come out from seeing the doctor so I could give him his card before he left but he was in with the doctor for a long time and I was beginning to think he had gone and I had missed him.

When he finally walked out of the treatment room, I waved at him to get his attention but he didn't look up and started to walk out of the waiting area and down the corridor. I ran after him, calling his name, and when he stopped and turned to face me I could see sadness and tears in his eyes.

I asked him what was wrong and told him I had a birthday card for him. He took the card from me and quietly said thank you, then he started to cry. I pointed to some chairs in the corridor and we both sat down. I grabbed his hand and pleaded with him to tell me what was wrong and, when he spoke, he started to shake.

Dr Wheeldon had told him the chemotherapy and radiotherapy had not worked as well as they would have liked and his cancer had spread and there was nothing more they could do for him.

I was shocked. I didn't know what to say. I just held my arms out to him and pulled him close to me and we both cried. When I looked up, I saw Jamie's dad walking towards us, his face was full of concern and, when he reached us neither of us spoke. I kissed Jamie on his forehead, stood up and turned to walk back into the waiting area for my appointment.

I was shocked and stunned. I couldn't believe what had just happened. Jamie had everything to live for. He was only a young man. How could he die of cancer? He had had the same treatment as I had and I thought maybe I too was going to die.

My appointment with Dr Wheeldon went by in a haze. He asked me how my treatment was going and gave me a new prescription for the creams, gels and mouth washes. He told me I had another week of this first session of radiotherapy then I was to have a four week break during which I was to rest and build my strength back up, ready to start the second session.

I walked out of the treatment room and I didn't mention to Dr Wheeldon that I was planning to stop my treatment. After seeing Jamie, I was now too frightened to stop. I knew I had to keep fighting and hope my outcome would be better than Jamie's.

I couldn't stop thinking about Jamie and all that treatment he had gone through and how it had all been for nothing. I felt it would be unfair if I survived and Jamie died and, in a way, I hoped I never bumped into him again because I would feel so guilty, knowing my treatment was continuing.

It was a massive reminder to myself that this could all go wrong and I could end up not surviving.

I started to make a list of things I wanted to do. I guess it was a kind of bucket list. I had done a lot of things and had completed a lot of personal challenges that I was already proud of, like running a marathon in Paris, seventeen days of back packing through the mountains in Norway, learning to ski and being quite good at it, until I got too confident and had my accident.

I had always been a good swimmer since my dad taught me how to swim in the river when I was five and at school I would win the races I was entered for.

Giving birth to my two daughters were the proudest days of all. To hold my babies in my arms and know they were created by me and their dad was an overwhelming feeling of love, a love I had for them from the minute they entered this world.

Now, when I look at some of the things on my bucket list, I wonder if I will ever do them

1) Get a tattoo
2) Go to Egypt and ride a camel
3) Snorkel the Great Barrier Reef
4) Canoe a hundred miles of a river
5) Climb the English Lake District fells again
6) Chase a Tornado
7) Stay in a haunted castle
8) Go to a music festival
10) Dance in the rain
11) Go skinny dipping
12) Make love on the grass in the rain
13) Ride horseback on a beach
14) Ride a roller coaster

15) See every member of my family and friends again

I had fifty things on my bucket list and, if Dr Wheeldon told me I only had months left to live, I would try my hardest to achieve every one of them, ticking them off one by one.

I went to the stationery shop on Park Avenue and bought some fancy stationery. The paper was a cream luxury quality with a small coloured butterfly in the top right hand corner of each sheet and the envelopes had the same. I bought a new pen, a Parker Fountain Pen costing $45 - a bit extravagant but I thought it was the right pen for the job.

Back in the apartment with my new purchases, I sat at the table and laid out four envelops in front of me and one by one I wrote each name in the centre of the envelope. Then I wrote letters to both my daughters, to Matthew and to my mum, only to be opened if I died. If I survived, I would tear them up.

It was the first time I had used a fountain pen since I was about thirteen years old and at school. Our English teacher, Mr Boyd, used to say using a fountain pen makes you write more slowly and makes you think more about what you want to write. I sat at that table for five hours writing those letters, each two pages long. They were very emotional to write and I cried the whole time I wrote them. When I had finished all four letters, I placed them in line next to the appropriate envelopes, then I picked them up and carefully read what I had written. I was pleased with the letters and the tidiness of the writing. The Parker pen definitely made a difference to their appearance. After sealing each envelope, I opened my briefcase with all my important documents in and I put the envelopes in the folder that had my birth certificate, knowing they would be found soon after my death.

Chapter Fifty Three

My four weeks' break started with me still being very sick. My mouth and throat were so sore I could hardly speak and I could only have cold drinks and eat soft foods.

I felt miserable and would spend all day feeling sorry for myself then trying to be cheery when Matthew came home from work, and being upbeat on the phone to my mum, Jessica and Melissa when they rang. It was amazing how I could convince everyone that I was fine and everything was ok.

I didn't tell Melissa about Jamie. I felt she didn't need to hear anything negative. I would write letters to my mum, never telling her how sick I really was. Instead, I would enclose photos of the progress of our new house and I would tell her what a wonderful life I was going to have living in such a luxury house and how I couldn't wait for her to come over and spend some quality time with me.

My mum would write back saying how nice the house was looking and how lucky I was to have the opportunity to have such a lavish life style. She would also say how lucky I was that I had gone to Canada because she felt I was getting better health care there than I would have in the UK. What she had forgotten was that, if I hadn't gone to Phoenix to get my cancer re-diagnosed, I wouldn't be getting any treatment.

She would always end her letters telling me she loved me and that every Sunday they were praying for me in her local church.

The last week of my four weeks' break I spent alone in the apartment. Matthew had to go to Houston on business and, as I was feeling a bit better, I didn't mind being left alone and I had planned for Jessica and Melisa to come over for lunch on one of the days.

Every morning, I wrapped up warm and made myself go out of the apartment and walk the river trails. Being the first week in November, it was cold outside around -15c and we had been having snow on and off since the middle of October.

The sun was shining and the snow on the trail crunched under my feet, while the cold breeze stung my cheeks and turned them a glowing red. I would walk all the way to the high level bridge then turn round and retrace my steps.

One day, I bumped into Barbara, who was walking along the river bank with her head down, covering the ground with her metal detector hoping to find some buried treasure. I had no idea how that thing worked with the snow on the ground, nor could I see the pleasure in it but she loved it and was armed with a little shovel ready to scratch away the snow to see what it revealed.

Barbara saw the fun in everything. She always made me laugh and I walked alongside her, laughing each time the alarm went off on the metal detector and she would find an empty pop can instead of something precious.

The anxiety I had about dying didn't leave me and, by night time, before I got into bed I would pray not only for me but for Jamie and his family. I never had a peaceful sleep. I don't think my mind knew how to switch off.

Chapter Fifty Four

Monday 13th November and I couldn't believe I was about to start the next round of radiotherapy. Knowing what to expect from the first four week session, I was feeling very nervous.

I had to see Dr Wheeldon first so I was at the cancer centre early. One of the nurses took some blood and checked my blood pressure and, when I went into Dr Wheeldon's treatment room, I was very worried about what he was going to tell me. Would it be the same as he had told Jamie? But he just explained again what was to happen on this round of radiotherapy and how the side effects would be different from the last time.

I sat very quietly, listening to what he had to say and, when he asked if I had any questions, I just said no. I just wanted to get on with it and get it over.

This time they were going to zap the area from underneath my breasts to the top of my legs, hitting my groin area and the same area on my back, making sure they were attacking every lymph node.

Once again, shields were put in place on my body and I was strapped to the bed so I couldn't move. There were two radiologists, both nice ladies, and they were very friendly and very good at putting me at ease. After setting me up on the bed, they walked behind a screen and pressed start and the machine did its job. Fifteen minutes later, I was out of there, saying see you tomorrow to the two ladies.

Towards the end of the first week, my skin became red again and sore, just like what happened on the first round of radiotherapy. Then I developed a cough and found I was out of breath a lot. I thought I was getting a cold and, by Saturday, I had a fever and didn't feel very well at all.

Matthew was very concerned when I wouldn't get out of bed on Saturday morning to drive out to the house to see it at a very interesting stage of dry walling the inside walls. The outside looked almost complete, with the roof on and the windows and doors in. The only things missing from the outside were the guttering and the taupe coloured siding.

But I couldn't move. I felt dreadful. Matthew called the emergency number and spoke to a nurse who advised him to drive me in to see them right away.

The cough was taking my breath away, leaving me feeling very weak, I saw the duty doctor when I arrived at the Kent Cancer Centre and, after checking me over and taking some blood tests, the doctor told me I had Radiation Pneumonitis, an inflammation in the lungs, which can develop when they are using radiotherapy in the mediastinal area. I told him they had zapped that area in my first four weeks and wondered why it had taken this long to get it. He told me it sometimes doesn't show up until a month or so after that area had been zapped. It was treated as serious and it was very important they got it under control so I was given cortisone medication to reduce the inflammation and, after they gave me some medication intravenously, I was allowed to go home as long as I rested over the weekend. Dr Wheeldon would check me on the Monday to see if I could continue with my treatment.

That was a tough weekend. My breathing was awful and I now knew how my daughter Jessica feels when she has an asthma attack and says she can't breathe.

Dr Wheeldon gave me the go ahead to continue my treatment then gave me another prescription for more cream for the burns and sores to my skin, as well as anti-nausea tablets. My cough was still there and I was still breathless but not as bad as I had been over the weekend.

By the end of that week I developed stomach cramps similar to severe period pains, due to them zapping away at my lymph nodes in the cervical area. I developed vaginal thrush and vaginal ulcers. I was in constant pain and was on medication to help. Dr Wheeldon advised me not to have sex as it would make it worse. Sex, what the hell was that? I hadn't had sex all year. Matthew showed no interest in that department and I couldn't blame him.

This wide field radiotherapy treatment was brutal. I was amazed how my body could cope with all this treatment and medication but I was struggling and, again, I wanted it all to stop, but every time I thought about it Jamie would come to mind and I would battle on, knowing I only had a few weeks left and hoping this was killing the rest of the cancer cells.

Chapter Fifty Five

Friday 16th December and after thirty one weeks, two hundred and seventeen days and five thousand two hundred and eight hours my treatment was coming to an end. This was my final treatment day and it was the most terrifying.

Going to the Kent Cancer Centre took up a lot of my time and, while I was there, I felt I was doing something positive about my cancer and now it was all going to stop.

I saw Dr Wheeldon before I went in for my last treatment and he assured me he thought everything had worked according to plan but they would know more in another six weeks' time, when I was to return for a scan. He said the radiotherapy would continue working in my body for another four to six weeks and I was to drink up to 3 litres of water a day to flush the dead cells out of my system and that peppermint tea was also very good for that.

I would also continue feeling unwell as the side effects would continue for the next few weeks and may even become worse for a period of time before they cleared gradually.

Tiredness was going to be my enemy and he told me that could last for another twelve months and I was to take multi-vitamins every day to try and rebuild my immune system back up.

He handed me an appointment card with a date and time to see him in six weeks and gave me a leaflet about a support group for patients who had just finished treatment.

When my treatment was over, I walked to my car and, before I turned the key for the engine to start, I looked out of the window at other patients driving into the parking lot then walking through the double doors into the centre. I felt so emotional and sad and, when I handed my parking pass back to George, the nice friendly retired English man at the gate, I told him that was my last day. He wished me good luck and said he hoped he wouldn't see me again and winked at me, before raising the barrier for me to exit and waving as I drove past him.

I drove home in floods of tears. The roads were so icy. It had been snowing all night and all morning and it was hard enough to see where I was going without my eyes being blurred with all the tears.

A snow plough was a few cars ahead of me and his flashing orange lights helped me keep the car going in the right direction. I parked my car in our allocated parking space in the underground parking bay at the apartment block and walked through the heavy metal fire door and, standing in the elevator, I pressed the button for the sixteenth floor.

I had no idea what I was going to do when I got in the little apartment but guessed the girls and Matthew would be desperate to hear how I had got on. I wasn't really sure I wanted to call them. I think I just wanted some quiet time to come to terms with how my routine was about to change again.

I put the key in the brown boring solid wooden front door of the apartment and in the hallway I removed my thermal gloves, woolly hat and scarf and my warm jacket and hung them all in the closet.

As I walked through the hallway to the living room I thought I heard something and slowly peered round the wall, afraid someone was in the apartment. There was someone there but nobody who was going to do me any harm. It was Melissa and Jessica, who gave a big cheer and congratulated me on it being my last day of treatment.

They were so excited, they had brought a bottle of champagne, some smoked salmon, cheese, pate and bread and made a special lunch, followed with a box of assorted luxury chocolates. I hadn't expected this and wasn't sure I was in the mood for it but I couldn't upset the girls. After all, year 2000 wasn't just a bad year for me, it was a very worrying time for them.

They had gone through the storage boxes in the spare bedroom and pulled out the

Christmas tree and boxes of decorations. We were due to move into our new house in the New Year so I wasn't going to bother putting the Christmas tree up but the girls wanted to make it a very special day and, with Christmas carols and songs ringing out throughout the apartment, it was a perfect day.

By the time Matthew got home from work, the girls had gone. They had drank the champagne while I sipped on one glass and they had cleared away what was left of the food and had eaten most of the chocolates but they left the apartment looking very festive.

It had been a long day and I was feeling really tired and not feeling too good from my treatment. I didn't really feel up to starting to explain everything to Matthew about what Dr Wheeldon had said so I went to bed and told him I would talk to him in the morning. Like most nights, I rolled about the bed from one side to the other, fluffing up my pillows and trying my best to get to sleep. A couple of weeks earlier Dr Wheeldon had wanted to prescribe me some mild sleeping pills to help me sleep but I refused them. I thought I had enough drugs going through my system without taking something to help me sleep. The downside of it was, the more sleepless nights I had, the more tired I got and the more tearful I became.

Chapter Fifty Six

Christmas came and I had to take a step back and let Melissa and Graeme make Christmas dinner. It was a lovey day but I found it so exhausting and I was glad when I could crawl into my bed as soon as we arrived home later that evening.

29th December and it had been a year since that terrible fall I had on the ski slopes in Jasper and I spent all day re-living every moment and counting my blessings. That fall saved my life. My broken back ended up being my lucky break. If I hadn't had that fall, I would never have known I had a cancer tumour and, by the time it was found, it could have been too late. Matthew was quieter than usual and he couldn't seem to concentrate on anything and I could tell it was also going through his mind.

It was snowing heavily outside but we didn't seem to notice it as we walked to Park

Ave and into Café Connect for lunch. We sat at a small table by the window and Matthew picked up one of the English newspapers, flicking through the pages while I sat looking out of the window. We didn't speak the whole time we were there. It was a very strange day and I wondered if, on that day every year, would we be feeling the same as we felt then.

Barbara and Ricky decided we were not going to sit at home feeling sorry for ourselves on New Year's Eve and were determined to make sure we had a good time. They had bought us tickets to go to the New Year party with them at Paddy's Irish Bar on Park Ave.

I must admit I wasn't looking forward to it but I took time with my make up and put my wig on, as my hair was still a mess from being bald at the back and thick on the top. After putting on the only black party dress I had, I actually felt I looked quite nice.

The bar was packed full of people, the women dressed in lovely glittery outfits and the men looking really smart, with most wearing shirt and tie, some with Dickie bow ties. Everyone had gone to a huge effort to be dressed for the party and the only seats we could get were stools at the bar.

There was an Irish band of four men and one girl all wearing kilts. They were jigging about the floor, dancing to the music and the whole place was dancing on the spot with them. It was a fantastic atmosphere and I was so glad we had gone.

Everyone in the bar counted down to midnight and on the stroke of twelve all five of the band members played Auld Lang Syne on the bagpipes, while the bar staff passed round glasses of champagne.

It was one of the most emotional New Year's Eve parties I had ever been to and walking back home Barbara and I couldn't resist the urge to make snow angels in the snow. Luckily for us it was only -18c and we were well wrapped up with lovely warm coats, hats and gloves.

Chapter Fifty Seven

10.30 Monday 15th January 2001 and I was sitting in front of Dr Wheeldon in his treatment room with Matthew by my side. I was there for the results of the CT scan I had had the previous week and the results from all my treatment.

It was a strange feeling knowing that the minute I walked into that room my life was going to change. I could get good news or I could be given a life sentence.

After Dr Wheeldon found out how I had been doing since my treatment had finished, which was well over a month ago and me telling him I was not suffering as much with the side effects but still feeling tired, he told me I had done really well throughout all my treatment and that he understood how difficult it was emotionally and physically to go through so much.

He then asked me if I had any questions and there was only one question I wanted the answer to and I asked him if I was cured of cancer. He told me he didn't like to use the word cured as that implies there is no trace of cancer left in the body.

He showed me the x-ray image from my scan, showing there was still a very little bit of the tumour left. It had started off the size of a lemon but was now the size of a small garden pea. I was disappointed as I hadn't expected to see any more signs of the tumour but he said he expected it to vanish over the next few weeks or it could just be scar tissue from the radiotherapy.

My treatment had been successful enough for him to say I was in remission but only partial remission due to still having a small trace of tumour left. I would have to continue getting check-ups every three months to make sure the tumour didn't begin to grow again.

Dr Wheeldon advised us to book a vacation, saying I needed time to convalesce and he thought we both needed time to relax and chill out together but there was only one place I wanted to book a flight for.

As I walked through the arrivals lounge of Glasgow International Airport, my brother Daniel was waiting for me and I couldn't run fast enough into his arms. Daniel and I had always been close and always there for each other and I wouldn't have wanted anyone else to be waiting for me at the airport.

He always knew how to make me feel good and, when he told me how stunning I looked, I knew all my effort had been worthwhile. Three days before my flight I had spent the best part of a day sitting in a hair salon having beautiful long dark real hair extensions attached to my short hair and, after washing and styling it, it fell half way down my back and shone in the light.

I had removed and reapplied my makeup on the plane before we landed and sprayed myself with the new perfume I had bought in the duty free shop. I was eating better now so my jeans were fitting me perfectly and with my lace black T-shirt and heeled shoes I felt so confident.

I could see my mum looking out of her living room window as we drove into the little cul-de-sac where she lived. I knew she was crying even before I saw her. Tears were streaming down my face as I couldn't wait for her to hold me. We had both waited all year for this moment and we were going to make the most of being together for two weeks.

My time with my family and friends back home (home is what I always called the UK.) went by so fast and I had a great time and made sure I didn't overdo it but there was one last thing I had to do before I flew back to Canada.

Sunday morning I walked to church with my mum. I liked going to church with her, it always reminded me of when I was a little girl singing in the choir.

We met the Reverend Heslop at the church door and he shook mum's hand then mine, telling me what a pleasure it was to see me. As we walked down the aisle, mum wanted to sit near the back but I led her to the third row from the front, where she got one of the biggest shocks ever. In that row sat both my brothers and my sisters-in-law. I made mum sit between my two brothers and I sat on the end next to Daniel.

The church was full and Reverend Heslop stood on the pulpit and started his Sunday morning sermon, ending by saying how privileged he felt to have such a special family in church that day. Then he welcomed me to the pulpit. The look on my mum's face was a picture and I nearly broke into tears knowing what she was about to hear.

Daniel squeezed my hand as I stood up from my seat and he whispered, "I love you Sis," and I walked to the front of the church and stood next to the Reverend.

I had written to Reverend Heslop as soon as I had booked my flight tickets to come home and he had written straight back, telling me how thrilled he would be for me to speak in his church.

I was shaking as I stood in front of the congregation. I am not one for public speaking but I felt this was something I had to do.

First I introduced myself and told them I lived in Canada and had returned to see my family after what had been a very hard year for all of us. I explained I had been fighting a personal battle with cancer and with a big ocean and thousands of miles between myself and my loved ones I believed it had been as hard for them as it had been for myself.

It was very rare for someone to stand up in church and talk about their fight to become a survivor of cancer but not so rare for people to talk about those who had died.

I told them I knew they had been praying for me every week in church while I was sick and I thought it would be good for them to see who that person was and to thank them personally for all their prayers as I do believe they helped.

I then turned to face my family sitting in the third row. My mum was crying and holding both my brothers' hands. I thanked each one of them for everything they had ever done for me and told them how much I loved them and how proud I was to be their sister, sister-in-law and to my mum her daughter.

I gave faith and hope to everyone who was going through their own battle with cancer and to their families and friends who were supporting them, as I knew how hard that battle was and, when I sat down, there wasn't a dry eye in the church, mine included.

Chapter Fifty Eight

June 2014 and every step I take is harder than the last. I am finding it harder to breathe and my heart is pumping fast with every breath I take. These steps are so hard to climb but I push myself to keep going. I look up and see the sun shining brightly in the blue sky and the path ahead is now in my sight and I know where I am going.

Climbing mountains is hard work and the Great Langdale valley is one of the best areas in the English Lake District for walking. It has a circle of steep sided mountains overlooking the valley and "Bow Fell," standing 3,440 feet high, has always been my favourite, with The Band, the first part of the ascent as it splits down the middle of the valley, making a steep walk over rocks like steps. It's a hard route up and has views that improve as you walk higher.

Those steep steps were the hardest part of the walk for me. With this section clearly out of the way, the climb became easier until we reach Three Tarn's where we had a rest and took in the excellent views down the Band into the Langdale Valley as well as across to most of the other Lakeland fells. From here we climbed rapidly over the Great Slab to reach the summit.

Sitting on the highest rock with the wind blowing all around me, the views were breath taking, looking across at the fell tops and miles into the distance with Scafell Pike, the highest mountain in England, standing high above the rest.

Ronnie handed me a cup of warm coffee from his flask and he knew what this meant to me today and we smiled at each other in silence. This is where I wanted my ashes to be scattered when I die so my spirit can blow free in the breeze. I never expected to get the chance to climb up here and feel so alive, knowing one day my family, possibly grandchildren, would climb up here and appreciate the views and honour my wishes but hopefully not for a good few years yet.

Having cancer changed me, it changed everything and I count my blessings for every day I'm alive.

It wasn't an easy decision to make to give up everything I had and return to the UK on my own in 2005. Sometimes in life you have to make choices that are right for you even though you know they will hurt the ones you love. Canada was never my home, the grass was never greener or richer for me and the pull to go home got stronger as the years went on.

One thing having cancer did for me was make me look at life differently, to know how precious every day is and how easy it can be taken from us. We only get one life and believe me, it's not a rehearsal, it's a constant challenge and sometimes a roller coaster ride but, to be truly happy and content, you have to be happy with where you are and what you're doing.

My partner Ronnie is the man I love to wake up to every morning and living in a beautiful part of UK makes me truly happy. I go to work each day in the local hospital working in the cancer unit, checking in patients for their daily dose of chemotherapy and I feel very happy, content, and thankful that I am alive.

The end

Printed in Great Britain
by Amazon.co.uk, Ltd.,
Marston Gate.